DAVID MCINTIRE

SWIMMING WITH THE SHARPS

A FOOTBALL SEASON SPENT IN LAS VEGAS

outskirtspress

DENVER, COLORADO

Swimming with the Sharps
A Football Season Spent in Las Vegas
All Rights Reserved.
Copyright © 2013 David McIntire
v2.0

Outskirts Press, Inc.
http://www.outskirtspress.com

ISBN: 978-1-4327-9954-0

Library of Congress Control Number: 2013914544

Outskirts Press and the "OP" logo are trademarks belonging to Outskirts Press, Inc.

PRINTED IN THE UNITED STATES OF AMERICA

Contents

Introduction

It was somewhere in southwestern Utah. I pulled off the interstate on an unseasonably cool summer afternoon just as large, cold raindrops started falling. Filling up on gas, a man sitting on the divider next to my car mentioned that my tire looked low. He worked at the little mechanic shop in the gas station so he told me to pull over to the free air pump next to the garage and he would top it off.

Like a lamb being led to slaughter I dutifully followed, concerned about driving another two hundred miles on a low tire. Sure enough, as he began to fill the tire he noticed cracks and thin spots. In his 'expert opinion' I needed to replace that tire before heading back on the road. In the grand tradition of men around the country who know little about cars but possess too much of an ego to admit it, I agreed. You know what comes next.

Well, it can't just be one tire, it needs to be both on the same axle. Oh, and now that we inspect the back tires they have the cracks as well. Best to change them as well.

Forty-five minutes and about $1,000 later, I was back on the road with four brand new tires. I felt full of confidence that no slick roads would send me careening off into a ditch but also felt a kernel of doubt eating at me that I had just been played like a Stradivarius.

I am a big believer in omens so it wasn't lost on me that it can't be good if on my way to gamble on sports for six months, I hand a bunch of money to a guy who knows more about a specific specialty than I do.

Three hours after leaving the gas station I drove into a significantly warmer Las Vegas and checked into my home for the next six months. The MGM Signature is connected to the MGM Grand sitting a couple blocks east of the Strip. The Signature consists of three buildings that house a mix of hotel suites and privately owned condos. I had rented a privately-owned condo, which makes me, in MGM's view, a third class citizen, like steerage on the Titanic--someone to be tolerated but given as little attention or service as possible. I would definitely be left for dead if the condo building begins sinking.

My condo consists of a bedroom, large master bathroom, guest bathroom, sitting room (with pull out couch) and a small but fully functional kitchen. Over the next six months I will spend countless hours sitting at the tiny glass table looking out the sliding glass door to my balcony, the landing strips of McCarran airport and the Spring Mountains beyond. It will become something like a home but that first night it just looked like another hotel room, something with which I am overly familiar.

As someone once said, the details of my life are quite inconsequential, but as your tour guide, I guess I owe you at least the outline of how I arrived at the MGM Signature Suite 7-814 in September 2012, ready to gamble away savings built up over a decade of hard work.

I grew up in Littleton, Colorado, a quiet, anonymous suburb of Denver that, after I left, would become best known as the home of one of the country's worst school shootings at Columbine. In 1993, I left Littleton behind and attended Florida State University in Tallahassee. Seven years later, I left Tallahassee having completed a varsity track career, an undergraduate degree, a Master's degree and my first year as an employee at a large management consulting firm. My soon-to-be wife, Jenn, a grumpy cat and I moved to Arlington, Virginia where we lived for three years before moving back to Denver in 2003.

Still with the same firm I joined out of grad school, our move to Denver signified a change in role for me that would put me on an airplane nearly every Monday morning. For the next nine years I spent nearly as much time in places like Dayton, Ohio, Purchase, New York and Seattle, Washington as I did in Denver.

All of that time traveling had a couple of results. First, I found myself with a lot of time to kill on airplanes, in hotel rooms and sitting in front of a computer, which led me to find the universe of writers on the internet. After a while, I realized I might want to try my own hand at writing, so after a couple short travel articles were published, I began writing a football-oriented blog.

There are positives and negatives to writing a widely-ignored blog read by a handful of friends and nearly no one else. You enjoy the freedom to learn and explore with no consequence. You can emulate your favorite writers. You can try pure satire. You can say what you think about anyone. But at the same time, you never find out if you are any good at actually writing.

By the June of 2012, my high pressure job was getting the best of me. I was frustrated and tired. I needed more of a break than a two-week vacation could provide. I also wanted to find out if all those hours putting my random thoughts into cyberspace had any benefit. I needed to answer the question, could I write?

As coincidence would have it, a couple friends and I had started a book club as an excuse to get together in football's off-season. One book chosen was *The Odds* by Chad Millman. Millman, now "ESPN the magazine's" editor in chief, spent a college basketball season following gamblers and bookmakers around Las Vegas. While reading, I was struck by how much Vegas had changed in the decade plus since the book was written. I also started to wonder what the book would look like in the first-person. What if someone goes to Vegas, not to follow the pros, but to battle them? What if I did that?

I had been taking annual trips to Vegas for the last few years to spend a long weekend playing blackjack and betting football so I knew the basics but, other than that, all I could bring to the table was years of football fandom and an embrace of my own ignorance. I could also find out what it is like to do nothing all day but write. I would continue posting on my blog, maybe pick up a freelance article or two to raise my profile and in the end somehow spit out a book. This book.

A seed was planted. The timing was right. I could ask for a leave from my job and get to Vegas in time for the football season. I could do this. I had some money set aside and have always felt it foolish to horde all of your savings for use when you are too old to do anything with it.

I floated the idea by Jenn who didn't immediately laugh at me. I floated the idea by my two friends who accompany me on those gambling weekends and they practically started helping me pack that day. Even my parents, who view a job as a blessing from the Gods, were encouraging. Most remarkably, my employer was agreeable.

This is where the second benefit of all those years in hotels for consulting engagements kicked in. It wasn't a daunting, overwhelming task to plan for six months in Vegas; it was just another project. Another city visited, another list of deliverables and a due date. Sure, this was the greatest project ever created, but it is still a project.

Before I knew it, the summer was gone, my career was on hold and my old Land Rover Discovery—overflowing with clothes, a bike, golf clubs and a computer—was heading west on I-70.

Apparently, heading west on balding tires.

The Basics of Betting

For reasons apparent to absolutely no one, when required to study a foreign language in high school, I selected German. I am not German. At the time, I had no plans to visit Germany. I had no reason for needing to understand German, outside of being able to understand what the Nazis said in Indiana Jones movies (mostly 'schnell' which means 'fast'; yep, still got it).

In a life of conforming to middle-of-the-road expectations, it was my one small rebellion against the system. Spanish and French were the expected languages. Latin was for motivated go-getters of which I was not one. German was the other choice.

After four years of schooling, I didn't use the language again for at least ten years – and even then it was just to annoy a German I met at training course for my job. Axel could speak four languages nearly fluently, yet whenever I pulled out the random elementary German word for him, he acted as impressed as a 1st grade teacher when a student correctly writes the entire alphabet.

Naturally, my first foreign travel was to Mexico on my honeymoon, a location where German was not exactly helpful in conversation. My wife, who had studied Spanish, and years of television taught me three or four words to get through some interactions; but, for the most part, I played the part of the ugly American assuming others always speak my language. We stayed at a resort catering to Americans so nearly all conversations could be had in English; but, maybe to help assuage the guilt of seeing the local village that had been bulldozed to build the resort, I tried my best to speak at least a few Spanish words.

Accustomed to crusty, wealthy Americans uninterested in communicating, the employees at the hotel would absolutely light up whenever a Spanish word was spoken. I remember once getting in a shuttle bus to return to the main resort from a golf course and greeting the driver with 'hola'. A broad smile creased his face and he immediately launched into rapid fire Spanish before I finally stopped him with my bewildered look and admission that I only spoke 'un poquito' Spanish.

It was my first lesson in the power of speaking the local language. Over the coming years, I would also go to Germany and France where I would try my best to occasionally embed a local word in the midst of my halting English.

Las Vegas isn't a foreign country – in fact, I argue it is the most American city– but that doesn't mean there isn't a new language to learn. The easiest way to stick out as a know-nothing in the sportsbook is to not speak the language. If you think a waiter in Paris is merciless when you don't speak the language, try placing a bet on a busy NFL Sunday without knowing how to do it.

Before diving in, I think it makes sense to give a basic outline of the language of betting. Sure, this is to help reduce your embarrassment when betting but it is as much laziness on my part. For the remainder of the book, I refuse to repeatedly explain short hand betting terms used.

Like Agatha Christie putting her cast of characters in an Index at the front to help readers keep track of who is a visiting duke and who is the valet, this chapter acts as the reference point to help translate any betting jargon to come.

Bet Types

Given the focus of this game is on betting football, I will concentrate on the types of betting done on football. Horse racing, baseball, even soccer have their own gambling peculiarities but I will ignore those for now.

For football, there are essentially three basic bet types: Point spread, Moneyline and Totals.

Point Spread Bets

The most common bet, the one quoted in your newspaper at home, is where the favorite not only must win the game but win by some determined number of points for a bet to win. For example, if the Patriots are six-point favorites over the Jets, the Patriots must win by seven for the bet to pay. Conversely, if the Jets lose by less than six or win, a bet on them wins. If the Patriots won by exactly six, it would be a 'push'--everyone gets their money back and no one wins.

The common way of showing this type of bet is to quote the favorite as minus the spread number and the underdog as plus the spread number. For example in the above game, in general you see this displayed as Patriots (-6) and Jets (+6). It can seem counter-intuitive that a favorite is shown as a negative number but get used to it; that is how things roll out here.

As a starting point, point spread bets pay $100 for every $110 bet for either team, which is generally quoted as -110. For clarification when I say 'pays,' this is in addition to getting the bet returned, so a correct $110 bet on the Pats pays $100 in winnings plus the return of the original bet, the bettor receives $210 in total. That $10 difference is called the 'vig' or vigorish which is essentially the casino's commission for granting you the privilege to make that bet. You are welcome. This spread ensures that if a casino saw the exact amount of money bet on each team in a match-up, it would still profit $10 for every $110 bet.

Money Line Bets

While a fancy name, money lines are the most basic bet in the casino. It eschews the point spreads and simply asks which team will win a game. It is easiest to remember that casinos can pull two levers to tilt odds toward themselves: points and pay outs. Move the point spread and keep pay outs the same (point spread bet) or move the pay out on a win and leave it at which team just wins (money line). In money line bets, favorites pay less than the money that you win on a point spread – the bettor on the favorite has 'bought' points. The underdog, in contrast, makes more.

These bets are always quoted relative to $100. For favorites, the money line is quoted as the amount that must be bet to win $100. For underdogs, the money line is quoted as the amount that is won on a bet of $100. Again the favorite is shown with a minus symbol, the underdog a plus symbol.

Going back to the above example, since Las Vegas believes that the Patriots are six points better than the Jets, a money line bet on the Patriots would be around -200 (the exact number being based on a number of factors). This translates that for every $200 a bettor lays on the Patriots, he would win $100. The Jets would be quoted around +180, which means that, for every $100 bet, a winning bet pays $180.

As with the point spread bet, winning includes the return of the original bet. If the Jets win and a bettor laid a $100 bet at +180, the casino would hand them $280, returning their $100 bet plus their $180 winnings.

Point spread and money line bets are the two most common and straightforward ways to bet on who will win a game. Deciding on which to bet is a personal decision. There are no hard and fast rules on when to bet which, unless you are a pro handicapper, capable of calculating whether the point spread or money line represent greater opportunity over their expected value. If you are reading this, that probably isn't you. It is all based on a bettor's personal beliefs about how a game will play out and how much risk they are willing to endure. Like any other financial market, higher risk means higher reward.

Think an underdog can win a game outright? Bet underdog money line and earn that extra pay-out. Unsure an underdog can win but you believe it should at least keep the game close, sacrifice the extra winnings and take the points.

Think a favorite will dominate? Bet the point spread, so you make (nearly) even money rather than a fraction of your bet. Uncertain the favorite can cover a spread but confident they'll win? Bet the favorite on the money line and sacrifice winnings for the added flexibility of needing them to just win.

Totals Bet

In contrast to point spread and money line bets, the total bet ignores which team actually wins and by how much. The totals bet simply looks at the total points scored in the game; adding Team A's score plus team B's score. Rather than posting different numbers for a favorite and underdog, the casino posts a single number and bets are placed on Over (combined score is higher than the number) or Under (combined score is less than the number).

Going back to our fictitious Patriots/Jets game, let's say that the Total number is 49.5. Like the point spread, the basic bet wins $100 or every $110 bet. If the final score is 28-21, a total of 49, those that bet Under win. If the final score were 35-27, those that bet Over win, regardless of which team scores 35.

Totals bets are best when a bettor is unclear on which team will out-perform the spread, but has a feeling about whether the game will be a high-scoring shootout or low-scoring defensive struggle.

While these are the basic options for almost every football game, there can be countless permutations in the sports book, especially for events like the Super Bowl where casinos will post hundreds of 'prop' bets. By definition, prop or proposition bets are wagers on something occurring not directly correlated to the outcome of a sporting event. For the most part, though, they take the form of either a money line where different prices are posted for two sides of a single bet (for example: will a team score in the first 6:30 of the game; Yes (-120) or No (+100)) or a totals bet where some over/under number is put up (for example – total yards passing by a quarterback: Over/Under 287.5 yards) and wagers can be made on whether that number will be achieved or not.

For the vast majority of games, these three are the only betting options available, with the option to bet either across the full game or just a single half; first half lines are posted before the game and second half lines posted at halftime.

As with most things, though, the simplest bets are just the beginning. Depending on your level of interest, effort and risk level there are many other considerations to make in betting. While prop bets add a completely new betting area, the two most common 'exotic' bets to make are parlays and teases.

Parlay

A parlay is simply a bet that multiple things will all occur. For example a bet that the Patriots, Broncos and Texans will all beat the point spread. For the bet to win, all three must win. If any of the three fail to cover the spread, the bet loses. As stated above, given the higher risk (and lower probability) of this occurring, the payout is increased. A basic payout on this to win pays around 6 to 1, though that payout varies based on the number of items in the parlay and the odds of those occurring. A $100 bet on this parlay would win $600 (handed back $700). Compare it to three separate $100 bets, one on each team. If all three won, those bets would win $272 on $300 laid (handed back $572). A parlay wins more on a smaller bet but if two of the three win, a parlay wins nothing while three separate bets would still win $181.

Parlays can be laid on any combination of the above options – combining separate games on point spreads, totals or even money line bets.

Tease

The cousin of the parlay is the Tease. Similar to the parlay, a tease bets on several different things all occurring. As stated above, there are two variables at play in sports books – point spreads and pay-outs. Where the parlay inflates the pay-out to offset the risk of multiple things occurring, teases adjust the point spreads. In football the most common tease amounts are 6, 6.5 or 7 point teases. These simply move the point spread by that amount. So if we assume the Patriots, Broncos and Texans are all seven-point favorites when put into a 6.5 tease, they all move to only be .5 point favorites--if they win the game the tease pays. However, you have sacrificed pay-outs for that moved line. In a $100 parlay, if those three all covered those seven-point spreads the bet pays 6 to 1. In a $100 tease the bet would only win $160.

Teases enable a bettor to reduce the risk of big spreads (or by betting on underdogs, increase a small underdog to a much bigger underdog) without paying the big premium of a money line. Teases are best used in conjunction with key numbers, a concept to be discussed much further later. In short, moving an eight- or nine-point favorite (who would fail to cover if they won the game by a touchdown) down to a 1.5 to 2.5 favorite, so that they cover with a three point win, is a great risk reduction strategy.

Understanding point spreads, money lines, totals, parlays and teases are enough for 95% of the bets anyone would lay on football in Las Vegas. But there are two last concepts to cover before you get your Gambling Degenerate 101 diploma.

Adjusted Juice

As discussed above, the standard vig is -110 on each side of a point spread or total bet. If a vig is not explicitly shown on a betting board, the -110 on each side is implied. However, as money starts to come in from bettors, the casino will adjust lines so as not to expose themselves to inordinate risk. If all of the bets come in on a favorite at -3.5, the line will climb to -4 and then -4.5 until money flows in on the other side. The casino doesn't necessarily want even money on each side but they also don't want all of the money on one side or the other.

Prior to moving the spread, though, the casino can try to shade bets to one side or the other by moving the vig. If a -3.5 favorite is getting more action than the underdog, before moving to -4 the casino can adjust the vig so that the favorite is now -120 and the underdog is +100. Now, bets on favorites must lay $120 to win $100. Bets on underdogs would pay $100 for every $100 bet. The goal is to entice bettors to bet the underdog by making the payout higher. If that still doesn't bring money on the underdog, the casino can then raise the spread.

While adjusted vigs don't necessarily impact how someone handicaps a game, it is important to recognize the impact it can have on winnings. Two bettors can get the same line but the difference in getting a bet at -110 and -120 is over $7.50 in winnings on every $100 bet. When a gambler winning 60% of their bets is a legend, sacrificing that much winning per bet can be the difference between profit and loss.

Reading the Betting Board and Placing a Bet

If you ask a bookmaker their biggest pet peeve, their answer will most likely be bettors incapable of reading a betting board and laying a bet properly. On a busy NFL Sunday, sports books don't have time to slowly walk novices through what all those numbers mean and how to place a bet. Bettors should walk to the window prepared to place their bet.

Let's start with reading a bet board. Here is a typical betting board for a single NFL game:

A	B	C	D	E	F	G
101	Jets		+100	49.5		-200
102	Patriots	-6	-120			+180

- **Column A** – This is the bet number. The unique identifier of each bet. It is this number that is used for placing the bet at the window

- **Column B** – The team names. The lower team is the Home team.

- **Column C** – The point spread. The team on the row as the number (shown with a minus) is the favorite. The other team is the underdog (the +6 is implied).

- **Column D** – the Vig on the point spread bets. Often this column is left blank which means both are at -110. In this example, the Patriots are six-point favorites, but you would bet $120 to win $100.

- **Column E** – The Over/Under number.

- **Column F** – The Vig on the Over Under. Here left blank to indicate -110 for each side.

- **Column G** – the Moneyline

Once you have found the bet you want to make and walk to the window, all that's required is to simply tell the bet taker what you want to bet. The easiest way to bet is to say the Bet Number (think of the number of games on a bet board, the bet taker hasn't memorized the number for each team, that is up to you) followed by the bet type and the amount.

As an example, if you want to bet $100 on the Patriots to win by more than six you would simply say:

"Number 102, with the points, for $100."

Betting on the Jets would just replace "102" with "101." You can replace "points" with "money line" or "Over" or "Under." Courtesy says to use the lower number for Under (so #102) and higher number for Over (#101) but in reality you can use either.

If you want to bet a parlay or tease, it is important to state this up front. A parlay of the Patriots and the Over would be:

"I want a Parlay of #102, the points and the Over, for $100."

For a Tease, it is the same as a parlay with the additional information of how many points you want.

"I want a 6.5 point tease of #102, #104 <Texans> and #106 <Broncos> for $100"

Looking at five or six boards, filled top to bottom with team names and numbers, can be almost overwhelming. The Soup Nazi-ish aspects of walking up to a desk and trying to properly annunciate the bet can be intimidating. Especially with an impatient bet taker and long lines of gamblers behind you trying to get their bets down before kick-off. That is why it is better to take a first attempt on a quieter day with less pressure to perform.

And never forget that everyone has to endure a first time. If it makes you feel better, Jay Kornegay, who now runs the LVH sportsbook, one of the biggest, most famous sports books in the world, told me about his first attempt to place a bet. Unfamiliar with the concept of the Bet number, he asked to bet on a team and ended up being scolded by a bet taker for not knowing how to place a bet.

First interactions in a foreign language are always awkward.

The Schedule

I'm not quite self-absorbed enough to quote the history's most famous civil rights leader to begin a book about casting aside all adult
responsibilities and spending six months in Las Vegas gambling and
writing. Instead, I shall quote one of the great musical anthems of ap-
proximately four months in the spring of 1993 and therefore my high
school senior class song.

I am free, to do what I want. Any old time.

I joined my employer two weeks after leaving the part time job I held
through grad school. Since joining the firm, the longest single chunk
of time I took off was three weeks, and even that included spots of
work.

Prior to the two weeks that marked the transition from grad school
student to full time employee, I don't think more than a week or two
passed without a full time job or school hanging over my head since
maybe the summer after my sophomore year of high school.

Basically, what I'm saying is that the first morning waking up in Las
Vegas was a strange, free and surreal experience. For weeks before
it started, I knew that the day would come when I walked away from
my job for six months and would no longer be checking emails every
day, and would not attend the occasional weekend conference call

or 6:00 a.m. meetings. But to actually realize it had happened was still unexpected. This plan had gone from theoretical pipe-dream to my day-to-day reality.

My job is writing and I'm gambling my savings on football and living in Las Vegas.

Some old consulting habits die hard, though, and not just integrating the phrase 'boil the ocean' into everyday conversation. I need a plan, an outline or target to work toward. I need spreadsheets to track how I'm doing.

I need structure.

I recognize that, at my core, I'm a lazy person. I don't do today what I can do tomorrow. If I'm not in motion, it is hard for me to get in motion.

From the outside this seems counter-intuitive. I always got good grades while competing in sports (and for periods in college also, holding a job). My job demands a lot of commitment and, by necessity, often comes before any other aspect of life. But I'm self-aware enough to recognize that without some sort of guidelines I could spend the next six months on the couch like Floyd from True Romance, watching bad TV and smoking out of a bong made from a honey bear bottle.

It is a balancing act though. I need to be productive but keep my schedule flexible enough so I don't burn myself out or end up writing the dullest book this side of instructions from IKEA. I won't hop myself up on amphetamines Jack Kerouac style – at least initially-- so I know I only have limited creative thoughts in a day. I can take breaks to run to the grocery store or go work out in the middle of the day but it's important to make progress almost every day.

My days are broken into chunks, divided by meals, because food is really the second most important thing in life, coming in closely behind morning caffeine.

I spend weekday mornings writing. After coffee, of course. Waking up between 7:00 and 8:30 a.m. (no alarm clock, which might go down as my favorite thing about this entire adventure), I make coffee, boot up the computer and begin searching the internet for the latest news and notes from NFL and college football. There are many, many internet sites that have already taken the trouble to scour for news and collate it into one place, why should I duplicate their work? Especially when they are on the East Coast and up hours before me? I generally go to: Twitter and then the major sports news sites, ESPN, SBNation and SI.com and review their news feeds and blogs.

While eating a bowl of cereal and beginning to fortify myself with caffeine, I finish reading and start writing. Sometimes this takes the form of short blog posts about the latest news of the day. Other times it takes the form of material that plays a dual purpose of being posted to my website while also forming the foundation of this book. If there is one thing that consulting taught me, it is that re-use is important. Why do something twice if it has already been done? So, if I can write something that can go on my site, as well as in this book, well, I am all for recycling.

With a couple things written, I make lunch and then read while eating and transitioning into my afternoon. This is when my day begins to diverge from the typical nine-to-five job. While others return to their cubicles and struggle through the post-lunch food coma, I mix things up. Early in the week, I spend my time handicapping, looking at lines and placing bets. When I find a few games about which I feel strongly, I will finish my sandwich and head down to the MGM sportsbook to lay my first bets of the week and (hopefully) cash any left-over bets from the previous weekend. Typically, these bets are the college games I feel most strongly about or ones about which I'm worried a line may move against me.

Other days, I get away from the computer and the sportsbook – either running to the grocery store or working out. Remember, I have no income, so despite being a short walk from Joel Rubochon, Tom Collichio and Emeril Lagasse's work, I can't dine with them every night. If not heading to the grocery store or sportsbook, I will try to work out to wake myself up and burn off all of those meals I so love.

The one day that doesn't conform to this rather boring and predictable schedule is Wednesday. During the majority of the football season, I carve a few hours out of my afternoon for a special project.

I go to the pool.

I don't just go work on my tan like a Jersey Shore cast member though. Instead I take this time to review every college football score and spread. Yes, it is as dull and tedious as you can imagine, documenting the scores and point spreads of every college game in the tables conveniently provided by Phil Steele's season preview magazine; but it has gone from an excuse to get some sun to become one of the best uses of my time all week.

What this little exercise gives me over the course of the season is a dedicated time with no distractions to really analyze how each team has done to date. Without a betting system as I use in the NFL (covered shortly), my college bets are based on tracking how teams perform relative to the expectations of the sports book each week and what I see with my own eyes watching games.

In the cacophony of a Saturday in a sports book it's impossible to track every game. It's hard enough to track the ones where a bet sits or involve teams still thinking about a national title. How can anyone accurately track every game from the ACC, SEC, Pac-12, Big-12, Big Ten, MAC, Sun Belt, WAC, Conference USA, Big East, Mountain West and probably some other conferences I have already forgotten?

Limiting betting to only the teams you follow for emotional reasons or because they are in the chase for a championship is a huge limitation in looking for value. The games that receive the most attention ultimately have the best point spreads. I like to think of each point spread as a rock in a river bed. Every bet acts like water flowing over the rock, buffing out any rough edges until only a smooth round rock remains. Those rough edges are value, so we want the rocks on the edge of the river in thinner, calmer water (i.e. fewer bets).

It is the games sitting in the shallows where value sits. The teams where I enjoy much of my success aren't in the top five; rather they come from second tier conferences like the MAC and Sun Belt. By quietly sitting next to a pool making these notes one team at a time, I have the time and information at my fingertips to notice that a Kent State or Marshall is consistently beating its point spread.

As the week progresses, with my initial handicapping completed, my writing also makes a shift from reviewing the previous weekend to forecasting the coming weekend. Right up until, before you even know it, that weekend is here when Thursday night games kick off.

During those Thursday night games, I also usually chat online with my friends, John and Rodney. We're partners in a weekly NFL handicapping contest and must reach consensus on the five games to pick each week. Three strongly opinionated football fans can require some time to come up with five agreed games, so we decided to do it with football on in the background (which also gives us something to discuss in and around our picks). They employ no system to leverage in making their selections, so opinions can vary wildly; but we ultimately always reach some common ground for picks. And when we don't, if the one that is ignored ends up being correct, the other two hear about it for the next week.

From a productivity standpoint my work-week ends around noon on Friday – another holdover from my earliest consulting days when I used to fly on Friday afternoons and the lesson was ingrained like with Pavlov's dog that Friday afternoons are not for work. By lunch on Friday, writing is done and my afternoon is spent laying any last minute bets, submitting our contest picks, running other errands or maybe heading to the golf driving range because all work and no play kind of defeats the purpose of living in Las Vegas.

Balancing writing and handicapping makes my schedule differ from that of a true dedicated handicapper. Where handicapping is part of my job, for them it is everything. They also spend a lot more time at it than I do. While I have a system I use, it is in no way as labor intensive or as all-encompassing as what a pro would use.

Steve Fezzik is one such pro. To give an idea as to what his schedule is like, here is what he describes as his work week in a 2009 interview with Statfox:

For me, you have to start on Sunday evening. Most professional gamblers I know are betting the halftime numbers on the late games and are preparing for opening numbers. For the very best players, there is no time to rest. They are not watching games to see how their bets turn out, though they may have them on, they are focused on the opening lines for the following week.

They are making their numbers for the following week on college and NFL games, so they are ready to bet as soon as the lines come up on Sunday afternoon. Because of their skill, they are able to get some really sharp bets. These bettors are not looking for in-depth analysis; they are searching for oddsmakers' mistakes. They are looking for numbers they know are off by two points. Any number that is off by two or more points and they think is obvious that anybody who does serious work in studying numbers, they will just fire (bet), even if the limits are low. They are going to hit what they see as mistakes.

On Monday, they are looking at props for Monday Night Football, looking to play a middle if available or fading a public move on the side or total.

Myself, on Monday I start breaking down totals on college football for the following week, since those numbers don't come until Tuesday.

Starting on Tuesday, everything to this point has just been my opinion. I will meet with a group of sharp bettors in Las Vegas and kick around thoughts and ideas, often focusing in on certain games and possible player injuries. This is the more intense handicapping day. If we are all in agreement, I'll shop for the best number and bet more on that game.

Wednesday is supposed to be an off day, but it seldom is, even if the lines have stabilized by this point. It's fairly typical for me to work until three in the morning Monday night and get up at seven a.m. on Tuesday. I try and sleep in on Wednesdays to prevent further sleep deprivation. Wednesday is usually date night and Thursday I return to handicapping looking for more particular advantages. I should add, in between I make any number of bets on games, be it sides or totals. Thursday my attention shifts to the various contests I entered and study the lines for what I might play. For me Wednesday, Thursday and Friday are similar.

Unlike the corporate world I temporarily departed, Saturday and Sundays are not free time in my new "job." It's time to focus on the games I have spent all week thinking about. It would be easy to dismiss weekends as days off when they consist of spending all day watching football--unless you have money riding on several games each week. When you're stressing about winning games from morning to night, calling it a 'day off' could not be further from the truth. It's exhausting. I often wake up on Monday morning more tired from watching twelve hours of football for two days straight than I did when I used to work twelve hours per day.

Following up with Steve myself to understand his gameday routine, here is how he described his Sunday and Monday, when he balances betting on games happening and getting ahead for the coming week's games.

Wake up. Spend 7:00 am-7:45 am with baby, often peeking at line moves early. Bet preflop games, halftime, and live wagering all day on Sunday nonstop. Frantically set lines for NEXT week's games. Bet THOSE at 4:30 pm at open. RUSH to a book or two MAYBE to bet Sunday Night Football props. Bet Sunday Night Football game live wagering all game. At end of game start watching NFL rewinds to see all games. Kiss baby good night. RUSH to books to bet late Sunday night games. Watch all remaining games on NFL rewind, pass out at 1:00 am after updating power ratings.

Monday am: Take care of baby 7:00 am-10:00 am. Watch remaining NFL rewind games. Update power ratings again. Injuries. Look intensely at situational spots. Start capping games 13 days from now to be ready to bet look ahead lines that come out Tuesday. Get College Football GOYS to my college guy, get his plays, bet them. Bet his recommended CFB plays. Bet any RAS college releases. Frantically go out to bet MNF props at properties. Bet live wagering all game. Kiss baby good night. Go to NFL expert's house, go over entire card, and who we like/share info. Often RUSH out to bet more games.

For a pro, the schedule is all about getting ahead of the games and getting bets at the optimal time. Steve mentions he starts handicapping games that are thirteen days away so that the moment a line is posted for those games, he is ready to bet if there is value. After a long day of watching sports, it is no one's idea of fun to make a frantic drive up and down the Strip to lay bets the moment lines open, but when every slight movement in a line can be the difference between long term profit and loss it is a necessity.

I am, of course, not at that level. For the most part by the time Sunday evening arrives, I am either depressed about losses or thrilled with wins. I start looking at the coming week's lines during the Sunday evening game but almost never lay a bet, having not yet run numbers through my system to determine where value lies. It won't be until late in the season that I am fully handicapping on Sunday nights and even laying bets on Sundays. Will this cost me money during the season? Undoubtedly. But some lessons must be learned the hard way.

Week #1

A Selection of my picks and rationale (written prior to the game)

South Florida (+2) at Nevada

Nevada is the darling of the casinos for the moment after their stunning win at Cal opening weekend. I get that a mid-major winning at the home of a BCS conference team is a big deal but Cal benched their starting quarterback for the 1st quarter and found themselves down 14-0. The rest of the way Cal outscored the Wolfpack 24-17. Cal had only 11 returning starters (6 offense, 5 defense) and the day was part of a grand re-opening of their renovated stadium (RIP: tree dwelling protestors). In short, Nevada was supposed to play the role of non-power conference patsy and get rolled by the big guys. Yeah, that was kind of rude to not play your assigned role, Wolfpack. I bet you left an upper-decker in the visiting locker room too. Get some manners.

USF on the other hand, opened with an easy win over Chattanooga and admittedly didn't use much of their playbook in doing it. With 15 returning starters (8 offense, 7 defense) from a team that opened with a win at Notre Dame last year, the Bulls won't be intimidated opening the season at the home stadium of a non-power team (you see what I did there?).

My initial Saturday morning starts early. The first adjustment coming to Las Vegas is moving to the Pacific Time zone. The Mountain Time zone is the ideal place to live as a football fan as far as schedule goes. College GameDays at 8:00 a.m. College game kick-offs at 10:00 a.m. NFL games kick off at 11:00 a.m. Early enough that your day is all football--there isn't time to start on errands before games kick off—but not so early as to require an alarm clock.

This means that the Pacific Time zone is just a touch too early for me. College GameDay starts at 7:00 a.m. Games kick off at 9:00 a.m. You are still sipping coffee when teams are on the way to halftime. Needless to say, without a strong reason I often don't exactly rush down to the sports book on Saturday morning. After a whole week of handicapping and laying my bets at the optimal time and place, what's the rush?

Therefore, even on the first Saturday, as excited as I am for the kickoff of my football season in Las Vegas, I don't rush out to the sports book. The games on which I have bets don't kick-off until around noon and, this early in the season, most of the games are nearly unwatchable annihilations of tiny schools in pursuit of a large paycheck. The games are on, but there is no reason to sprint down to the sports book.

USF was my biggest bet of the week, having laid bets at both +1.5 and +2, so I timed my initial trip to the sports book to coincide with watching the game. Given it is only my first weekend (though the second of the college football season), I decided to start close to home at the MGM.

The MGM consists of a long thin, slightly bending band of TVs and seats bisected by one of the main thoroughfares connecting the casino to the Strip. The majority of the seats are rows of theater seats with the wooden arm rests we all had in elementary school. A second set of more lounge-y chairs and couch/benches line the back wall. A section to the side with individual cubicles is focused on horseracing. There is also an upstairs VIP section of dedicated boxes, like you find at a stadium.

The broad wall possesses a large number of TVs of varying sizes, as well as the bet boards, providing a nice single stop for almost any game and bet. All of the TVs are HD and spread out the length of the wall, meaning if you want to watch a game on a small TV you'd better hope you find a seat in front of it.

The long flat area dictates the seating – individual seats spread out in a row. The only area where a group can sit in a circle or cluster is in the back (or VIP) but the challenge is that the walkway is between the couches and the wall, meaning your games are interrupted by a constant stream of people carrying yards of alcohol stumbling in from the Strip.

Given its central location and relatively tight size, the MGM is almost always packed if there are games on. On a Saturday, if you aren't in a seat by noon, you will be begging for a seat or squeezing in next to others.

By the time I got to the MGM sports book in the middle of the 1st quarter, the Bulls were trailing 14-0 and I needed a beer. Immediately.

After the half, USF scored to make the score 21-20 and, more importantly, cover. By forcing a three and out on the next drive USF had grabbed momentum...right up until the punt returner muffed the punt and Nevada recovered.

Oh waitress…

As the clock wound down in the fourth quarter, Nevada had opened up an 11-point lead: 31-20 and I was still waiting for the waitress to appear with the beer I had ordered after half (MGM sports book wait staff = not fast). USF scored with 4-5 minutes to play (I was too far from the tiny screen to see the actual clock) but failure to connect on the 2-point conversion cuts the lead to 31-26. On the ensuing Nevada drive, USF held the Wolfpack offense to a punt after only a couple first downs.

USF got the ball back deep in their end with around a minute to play (again, I couldn't see clock. The added stress of not knowing the time left did not help). A couple first downs got the ball up to near field when USF quarterback, B.J. Daniels decided he was tired of completing 10-yard passes and launched a long pass down the sideline.

To be perfectly fair, Daniels had been launching ill-advised long passes all day with little to no success. Clearly, he thought the bigger, faster USF WRs could beat the Nevada secondary but for the most part had nothing to show for it. And wasting at least one down on a hail mary when you only have three downs to get a first down tends to limit success. Not that I was bitter.

This time, with the game on the line, as the ball fell back to Earth the Nevada cornerback in coverage stumbled and USF wide receiver Andre Davis cradled the ball and coasted to the end zone. Another failed 2-point conversion left USF clinging to a 32-31 lead with about 30 seconds left (I think). At this point, a Nevada field goal would push one of my bets and lose my other (oh, and I guess USF would lose the game too, but whatever). Thankfully, after a couple first downs, a sack at midfield ran out the clock and the Bulls held on for a huge win for me.

USF's win came at the same time as another win, as Iowa State took the Cyhawk trophy from Iowa. My only loss of the day came when Wyoming was beaten at home in Laramie by Toledo. Nope, I don't know how it happened either. Maybe LeBron played for his hometown team, Toledo.

Four hours after arriving, I took a break from the sports book to clear my lungs and eat some dinner but soon enough I was back to watch the Vanderbilt/Northwestern game.

High on the USF and Iowa State wins, I decided to roll over some money on a night game, betting on Vanderbilt (-3) at Northwestern, something every expert warns against; if you didn't see value before a wins or losses on other games, there isn't value now. It is one of the cardinal rules of handicapping and one I break more often than the speed limit.

It seemed to me that Vandy's tough loss to South Carolina was undervalued relative to Northwestern's high scoring affair in Syracuse. In hindsight, Syracuse's shootout versus USC earlier in the day should have been the hint that Northwestern's week one game was better than I was giving it credit for.

Vandy clung to a late 10-6 lead (and cover) in the fourth but Northwestern's offense was moving much better in a driving rain storm. Northwestern finally broke through and scored the go-ahead touchdown. Vandy running back, Zac Stacy, responded by breaking a long run down the sideline. The offense stalled inside the ten and a field goal tied the game at 13-13.

Northwestern marched right back down (Big Ten wearing down the SEC? Travesty) and kicked a field goal to take the 16-13 lead. On the first play of the ensuing drive, with about a minute to play, Vandy quarterback, Jordan Rodgers, was sacked and fumbled to a Northwestern lineman. A salt-in-wound touchdown sealed it but I was too busy deciding whether Rodgers (Aaron's little brother), was more Ozzie Canseco or Billy Ripken to care.

(I lean Ozzie, since I own the infamous Billy Ripken "F**k Face" baseball card which will make me money when I sell it, unlike Rodger's abysmal performance).

After the game I went back up to my room with a head light from stress and too many oversized beers, a neck sore from staring up at the TVs on the wall and lungs clogged with hours of second hand smoke. Despite the Vanderbilt and Wyoming losses, I finish the day in the black so my bankroll is in much better shape than my body.

Maybe my bankroll will make it to the end of this little experiment after all. As long as my body does too.

Lions (-7) vs Rams

I will admit it – I don't get this line. I am 93% sure that these words will come back to haunt me on Monday, but I don't see how this line makes sense. When I predicted a line for this game before looking at the spread, I came up with Lions -11. This opened at -9 and has moved down to -7. What do the experts see in the Rams that I don't? I may like Sam Bradford more than many people but with his only weapon being Steven Jackson, how does he move the ball with the likes of Nick Fairley and Ndamakong Suh in his face. I think the Rams defense will be improved – they were ranked 26th in points allowed last year, so there is really only one way to go – but I don't know how they slow down the Lions' passing game. Even with no real running game, the Lions could put 31 points. Heck, if Calvin Johnson were playing the Lions one on eleven, I would still install him as a 2-point favorite.

This line seems so obviously incorrect, I am definitely wrong about it.

Sunday morning, I decided to go to the LVH, formerly the Las Vegas Hilton, for Football Central. Football Central is LVH's dedicated theater showing only NFL games on eleven HD screens. Featuring free admission with no age restrictions, drink and food specials and no smoking, Football Central draws locals and vacationers, alike, every Sunday morning for their particular brand of worship. It is the kind of place where someone not wearing a shirt espousing their favorite NFL team is viewed by all the other parishioners like someone arriving at church in jeans--with a mix of condemnation and skepticism.

Making my way past the displays of merchandise and grabbing a raffle ticket, I entered the dark theater of Football Central and found a seat near where the Lion's game was being broadcast among the other morning games. I wish I had instead sat as far from the game as possible.

You should seriously begin to question your mindset when you have an internal debate for several minutes about which STD a quarterback may have contracted that would explain his horrendous performance. But such are the depravities that result from gambling.

Or more specifically gambling on Matthew Stafford.

I landed on syphilis, if for no other reason than the fact that it is a fun-sounding word, and it seems reasonable that it could cause horrendous decision making and poor passing accuracy. I mean have you seen any of Paul Gauguin's art? Does that look like the work of a man capable of completing a 15-yard out from the far hash mark?

Now, to be clear, I'm not actually accusing Stafford of contracting syphilis (stand down, lawyers), I'm just trying to find a rationale for his epically awful performance against the Rams. I watched pretty much every moment of this game (until the last minute when I got up in disgust), and it was pretty clear the Lions were the vastly superior team.

First downs: Detroit - 28, St. Louis - 14.

Total yards: Detroit - 429 yards, St. Louis – 251

Yet, somehow they needed to score a TD in the final twenty seconds to salvage a 4-point win. What kept this game from being an easy cover for the Lions? Matthew F. Stafford.

(I have no idea what his middle initial is but it will be F for me from now on – use your imagination).

A dominating drive to open the game, including a surprisingly strong running game (4.6 yards per carry on the game) – the biggest question mark for the Lions – ended with Stafford throwing an interception on a short receiver stop at the goal line.

Holding a 7-6 lead late in the first half with a chance to drive down and go up 14-6 before half led to a pick-6 for Cortland Finnegan on yet another out route and a 13-7 deficit.

Should we have seen this coming? Should we have expected Stafford to do his best early-career Jay Cutler impression? In his career (31 games), Stafford has thrown for three or more interceptions five times. Three of those came his rookie year. The others came last year against two solid defenses that are familiar with him (Chicago and Green Bay) – not a mediocre defense, at home in his fourth season against a team that was 23rd in the league last year in turnover differential.

The logical argument is that the arrival of Jeff Fisher's moustache in St. Louis was the difference last year, but I just didn't see it. As stated above, the Lions were the much better team. Their quarterback was just sloppy with the ball and kept a team alive that should have been done at the half.

Not a positive start to my Sunday.

Fresh off the morning Lions loss and still at the LVH for the afternoon games, I decided on a whim to recoup some losses with an ill-advised parlay of first half bets on the Over in the Green Bay/San Francisco game (23.5) and Seattle (-1) at Arizona.

The logic of these picks was that I only needed a 14-10 game in Green Bay for that cover, and with Green Bay's high powered offense, that seemed very doable. I did not expect the overwhelming Niner defense to almost completely neuter the Packer offense. Even though the Niner offense did its fair share, this ended up falling .5 point short when the Niners took a 16-7 lead into half.

On the other pick, I expected the Seahawks defense to completely smother a shaky Cardinal offense. I mean...John Skelton...seriously? With Seattle rookie quarterback, Russell Wilson, starting I thought the Cardinal defense may require some time to adjust to stop a player that they don't have much film on. I thought the Seahawks might be able to get up early and then have a battle in the 2nd half to retain the lead.

Unfortunately, the Cardinals defense is better than I gave it credit for and the Seahawks offensive line left Wilson running for his life as much as anything else. One or two drives by Skelton were all the Cardinals needed to lead 10-3 at the half.

I crawled back into the afternoon heat having lost repeatedly. All of the positive feelings from Saturday had been undone. Twice I placed a last minute bet on a late game to either add to my winnings or rebound from a loss. Both times I failed miserably. An important lesson to remember.

For almost 24 hours.

I finally got an NFL win the next night - winning a bet on the Ravens facing the Bengals on Monday night – the gambling equivalent of that one great golf shot you always hit at the end of a bad round that brings your back to the course again.

Running down to the MGM book to cash my Ravens ticket and lay a couple college bets before the lines move against me, I decided to also watch the 2nd half of the Chargers/Raiders Monday night game. Sitting in the book, staring at this line, I decided to throw a small 2nd half bet on a parlay of the Under (23.5 points) and San Diego (+.5). The only positive about parlays are that they are a way to win a decent amount with a small investment (this paid more than 3 to 1). Of course, that also means the casinos (who ALWAYS know more than you) think the odds of this hitting are slim.

I kept this amount small enough that it wasn't a real hit to my bank roll but would pay a decent amount if it did come through.

My logic: Unlike the parlay above, laying this bet at halftime gave me a first half of precedent to watch. What I had seen was two defenses demonstrably better than the offenses (halftime score was 10-6 Chargers). Having seen two good offenses fail to score 24 in a half on Sunday afternoon, it was hard to imagine these two offenses suddenly awakening and rolling off a bunch of points – ultimately they combined for 20 points with one score being a last minute Raider touchdown with the Chargers in full-on prevent mode as they nursed a two touchdown lead.

I parlayed with the Chargers because after a half it was clear the Chargers were the better team. The Raiders' offense still had the same issues as the last few years (it goes by the name 'Carson Palmer and a bunch of receivers you have never heard of'). With the Chargers +.5, I basically assumed a better Charger team would score as many points as a disappointing Raider team. The first half had told me they would.

The Chargers outscored the Raiders 12-8.

Was it a bet probably best not made? Yes. But it was a win at nice odds, off of a minimal investment, so it was just the sprinkles on the ice cream of opening weekend.

And Matthew Stafford wasn't involved in any way.

The System

When it comes to trying to survive sports gambling, there are important factors to consider and then there is the system. A gambler's handicapping system is like the Holy Grail from Indiana Jones and the Last Crusade: pick the right one and you are set for life; choose poorly and you are dead. If you ever do find it, you can be sure others will be right behind you and won't be above violence trying to wrench it from your cold, dead hands.

So, it's kind of a big deal.

When your job is to try to win more often than you lose gambling against casinos, the system you use to guide your gambling is the only chance at winning consistently. Any dumb schmuck can win occasionally (<looks deeply in mirror>) but to beat casinos consistently takes a point of view that differs from how the casinos look at the game.

Have you seen these casinos out here? An ancient Egyptian Pharaoh would behead an entire village out of envy if he saw these monuments to ego. Opulent palaces built at such a scale it's easy to envision some well-meaning father dragging his pale Midwestern family to a painful sunstroke death as they stroll the Strip to the next casino because 'it is just up there.'

In the mountains, they warn of foreshortening in which mountains appear smaller and closer than they really are because of the scale of the surroundings and lack of a true, flat horizon. In Vegas, the same problem exists, only it is man-made and located in a desert valley where autumn temperatures can top 90 degrees.

The one common denominator tying the Luxor pyramid, Paris, New York-New York, Bellagio and Palazzo together is not the base cultural stereotypes on which they are built, it is the money required to build them. And, if it isn't obvious, the casinos of this size aren't built by losing bets. Casinos aren't a charity. Casinos employ the most sophisticated fool-proof tools to minimize the risk of losing bets. Of course there is always risk, but with the high data mining capability of computers today, casinos can find ways to minimize their exposure while ensuring there isn't a lock of a win available, despite what all those guys on the internet say.

This is where the system comes in. As we all learned in WarGames twenty years ago, there are always ways around any computer program. Math is only as good as its inputs. If a wiseguy can find the right combination of mathematical factors, he can potentially find a back door that will lead to the casino's own version of Global Thermonuclear War: consistent, big losses.

Wiseguys typically spend years sharpening and honing their systems and the underlying factors but in the end they usually result in the same basic components:

1 – Power Rankings – a ranking of each team from best to worst with each team's relative strength to each other. For example, Team #4 is obviously better than Team #5, who is in turn better than Team #6. But the key is defining by how much. This may not seem all that important, but, to employ an outrageously oversimplified example: Team #4 may be 4 points better than #5 but #5 may be better than #6

by only 2 points. What if Team #4 played Team #5 last week and was favored by 3. This week Team #5 plays Team #6 and is also favored by 3 points. Which game is a better bet for the favorite and which is a better bet for the underdog? Without relative strengths you might as well go with which mascot would beat the other in a fight. Given how bad the CU Buffaloes have been the last few years, this is clearly not a winning strategy.

2 – Projected Line – With the power rankings in place, a 'true' point spread can be assigned for each match-up and compared against the offered point spread to determine if it has value. In the above example, if next week Team #4 is playing Team #6, the power rankings would expect Team #4 to be a 6-point favorite, plus or minus the home field advantage that is typically assumed to be worth three points in the NFL. Significant deviations from this expected spread offered by the casino identifies the best betting opportunities.

3 – Bet amount – Multiple strategies exist for determining how much to bet but, in the end, the only way to beat a casino consistently is to bet big when the odds are the best. This is true across an entire casino, not just in the sports book. Counting cards at blackjack – after stripping away all of the nuance and accepting the basic mathematical probability underpinning it - follows this same philosophy. The bettor seeks the moment when the odds are most in his favor (when there are a disproportionately high number of face cards in the deck), and bets the most. When odds are lowest (disproportionately low number of face cards in the deck), bets are reduced.

To accomplish this in the sports book, the wiseguy develops a strategy that correlates the difference between his expected line and the casinos posted line to a wager level. The higher the difference, the higher the probability of success, the higher the wager.

This is why the system is treated with more care than the Crown

Jewels. Every bet is based on the system. If a bettor's power rankings are wrong, then so is the relative strength of a bet versus the line posted, and the larger wins needed to be successful long term are back to being a coin flip.

The natural question here is to ask what a pro bettor's system actually looks like. Good question but not so easily answered. Systems are the most closely guarded secrets in Vegas outside of where all the Cirque de Soleil people come from. As part of an interview with professional gambler, Steve Fezzik, I asked him about his system. Here is the entirety of his response:

Pretty simple. Have power ratings, set lines. Adjust for situational spots. Bet anything that's off. Also do my best to forecast line moves.

Yes, pretty simple.

You could laugh at the secrecy with which handicapper's guard their systems; just because someone else places the same bet he does, doesn't mean he is going to lose. This isn't poker – one bettor's win is not another bettor's loss.

However, this reasoning, while technically accurate, ignores the fact that point spreads are a moving target. Like everyone buying a stock, spreads react to the market. If everyone uses the same systems and reaches the same conclusion then it is a race to see who gets their bets down before the spread adjusts. It is better to be the only one identifying the right bets.

Also, it should be noted that for someone like Fezzik, secrecy is even more important. There are people that impersonate him on the internet and sell picks using his name and the reputation he has built up over time. He also offers picks for a fee on his website. If everyone knows how he arrives at his picks, then his business disappears overnight. For Fezzik, his system is his livelihood, so you can understand why he protects it with the ferocity of the guys guarding the briefcase in Pulp Fiction.

Which brings us back to my little experiment. I don't have the knowledge and money to spend what the casinos or pro handicappers do. Nor do I have years to refine my system and I refuse to just use other people's picks. My arsenal is limited to years of fanatical football fandom and some experience with small wagers on regular trips to Vegas with buddies. It's like calling up a weekend softball league player and asking him to hit major league pitching. Best case is him escaping with his life.

I may not have millions of dollars riding on each of my bets, but I still need a base quantitative system to use. Because I don't have millions riding on it, and this is a short term gig only, I am free to share my approach here.

Besides, if you are trying to steal my system, God help you.

No matter how rationally a person views himself, we all have built-in biases--both conscious and unconscious. There is a good reason that quantitative analysis has taken over sports in recent years – it removes these biases that cloud what is really occurring. It isn't a co-incidence that sports bettors were years ahead of teams themselves in using math to define better teams; when you have your own money at stake you will look for any edge that improves the probability of winning. A human can't help but remember a team getting blown out last week. A spreadsheet appropriately balances that for what it is - a single data point. It is then up to the bettor to find the context for the blow out. Was there a schematic advantage for the other team? Was a key player hurt? Was it just the bad luck of a bad bounce or two? Quantitative systems help find more insights to help balance what our memory holds of a game.

There are some handicappers who don't even believe in watching games; they are completely reliant on what their systems tell them. They know that their eyes can lie, so they remove them completely from the equation. I can't go this far. I actually have the opposite opinion personally. I believe that watching teams--their strengths and weaknesses--is important to answering some of the contextual questions above. However, I also recognize that simply trusting eyes and guts mean you are always playing last week's games, not this week's game. I need a system to start from. I may not follow its direction word for word, probably to my detriment, but I still need a foundation to build from. But how to build a system on short notice?

One of the first lessons drilled into your head when working for a large consulting firm is to not reinvent the wheel. Most likely, no matter what challenge or problem you face with a client, someone somewhere has faced a similar issue. There is no reason to spend hours building some complex solution without first tapping into the existing base of knowledge already out there in the firm.

(If you are a corporate executive responsible for hiring consulting firms, please ignore the above paragraph because you are special. Your consultants recognize that the challenges you face are unique and would never re-use knowledge from other clients. Those high hourly wages you are paying them are totally worth the completely unique and ground-breaking work they are doing for you. It is every-one else who gets recycled solutions).

With that background in mind, recognizing I need a power ranking of NFL teams and having only a few days until the NFL season kicks off, I decided to find people smarter than me and leverage their work. I chose to focus my system on the NFL, given the smaller universe of teams and relative competitive balance. I will continue using the old fashioned eye test on my college bets; think of it as the control group of this little experiment.

Football Outsiders is a group that is cutting edge in looking at football statistics in new and interesting ways. They are basically trying to apply the Moneyball approach to football and have been doing it for years.

In other words, maybe a lazy writer with limited math skills can leverage their work to short-cut his way to a profitable gambling system.

One of the key concepts that Football Outsiders has developed is DVOA or "Defensive adjusted Value Over Average." Without going into the depths of DVOA (better explained on Football Outsiders web site itself), DVOA looks at each play in a game and grades how successful it was relative to average outcome for that play, adjusting for the defense played, situation, etc. The result is an ability to define how much better or worse each team is in totality compared to a wholly average team. As Football Outsiders, themselves state:

DVOA has three main advantages over more traditional ways to judge NFL performance. First, by subtracting defense DVOA from offense DVOA (and adding in special teams DVOA), we can create a set of team rankings that's based on play-by-play efficiency rather than total yards. Because DVOA does a better job of explaining past wins and predicting future wins than total yards, it gives a more accurate picture of how much better (or worse) a team really is relative to the rest of the league.

Which sounds a little like a power ranking to me.

DVOA was not created as the basis for a gambling system (in fact, F.O. has their own predictive betting system to which one can subscribe that I'm sure is more complex than anything I put together) but for my purposes DVOA meets the goals I have for the foundation of my system: (1) rank all of the teams in the NFL in order of strength and (2) define the difference in relative strength between each team.

With a foundation in place, I then need to determine the best way to apply those power rankings to each game's point spread and determine where value lies.

As noted above, a wiseguy's system will not only rank these teams but also apply the 'correct' point spread to each game. With limited data to work with and no off-season to refine the system, I don't have that luxury, so I instead take an alternative approach.

By simply looking at the difference in two team's DVOA rankings relative to the defined point spread, I can have an overly simplified look at where the difference in relative strength (DVOA) is most different from the point spread being offered. Large gaps in DVOA rankings relative to small spreads equate to value.

For me, though, this is only the beginning. Recognizing the limitations and simplicity of this system means then applying a level of intelligent design to the bets. For example, teams with higher DVOA playing on the road are regularly overrated by this system (due to the reduced spread resulting from the other team's home field advantage), so this is where things get a lot less scientific.

Match-ups, momentum, history, performance in similar situations – items usually classified as anecdotal evidence – can be applied as the tie-breakers. There is also another, completely separate level of quantitative analysis to be completed.

There are really two types of quantifiable analysis to be completed for a game; (1) analysis of the team's performance on the field or (2) analysis of the team's performance in the casino.

The first involves looking at playing statistics – offensive yards per game, yards per pass completion, turnovers per game, etc. This is the component where I rely on smarter people from F.O.

The second involves looking at how the team's performance in games has translated to performance in the sportsbook. How has a team done against the spread? It matters less whether a team actually wins a game but do they consistently beat the point spread set on them? It is this perverse view that can lead wiseguys to love a 4-12 team much more than a 16-0 team.

Thanks to the abundance of data just a browser window away, against-the-spread data can be found for teams at not just the highest level but also sliced and diced in more ways than are available on a late night TV infomercial. Against the spread performance, home, away, at night, during the day, on turf, on grass, in different months of the year, is all available with a couple simple mouse clicks.

My system will certainly not reinvent football betting, nor will it keep a casino from adding on a new wing, but maybe it will provide enough of a combination of quantitative foundation and intangible dusting to let me occasionally find real value.

As I said, this system is designed for the NFL. I do not have an equivalent system for college. I am going 100% gut on this one (well, let's say 90% gut – sort of like Mark Mangino - there are still a few tools out there to leverage). With less data and more teams, college bets will be based on what I see with my eyes and the research I can conduct each week on how these teams have done against the spread to date.

Week #2

USC (-9) AT STANFORD
This line has been all over the map this week. It opened at -9.5 and I worried about it jumping over the 10 point mark (thanks to USC's popularity and the whole 'might be the best team in the country' thing). I rushed down to the MGM book on Monday night and locked

in at -9.5. Naturally, the next day it was down to -8 (and even -7.5 at some books) after USC's senior, All-everything center, Khaled Holmes, was injured last weekend and it was reported he may miss this game. Reports are still murky on whether Khaled will play because Lane Kiffin is that rich kid from every '80s teenager movie that everyone hates for being a prick.

I don't know if Holmes will play, but I do believe USC will win handily regardless. After giving up 29 points to Syracuse last week in a strange game (interrupted by rain on multiple occasions, played in New Jersey), it is easy to believe the USC defense will be their Achilles heel and that Stanford's pro-style efficient offensive machine will match USC's high powered offense.

I don't believe it. I think USC comes out with a point to prove against a team that beat them a year ago. Yes, Stanford put 50 points on Duke last week but....Duke. Still young at quarterback and across the line, I don't see Stanford being able to hang with the Trojans and after USC takes a 21 point lead in the 2nd quarter, the raucous crowd will quietly slink back to the computer lab – those jobs at Apple and Google aren't going to fill themselves.

#2 – NORTHWESTERN (-4) VS. BOSTON COLLEGE

Last week, Northwestern beat Vanderbilt and cost me money in the process. Is this overreaction to a loss? Maybe. But then that is to believe Boston College could go into Evanston and beat the Wildcats. Or even to believe in Boston College at all. This is a Boston College team that lost at home to Miami in week #1 before beating up on Maine in week #2. Miami then went to Kansas State and lost 52-13. Boston College has yet to leave the friendly confines of Chestnut Hill. Prior to knocking off Vandy (SEC! SEC! SEC!) last week, the Wildcats won in Syracuse the week before.

Northwestern is a solid team and Boston College is spending their weeks scouting Big East assistants to hire as their next head coach rather than scouting their opponents. You may think Frank Spaziani has a play sheet in his hands but it is actually his resume, ready to hand out to any big money donor or university official he may meet from an opposing team. There is a 57% chance this approach will get him hired as Maryland's next head coach after BC plays the Terps later this year. But it won't help against the Wildcats.

With the preponderance of games on Saturday afternoon and evening I decided to go out and explore beyond the MGM. Rather than going somewhere new, I instead returned to my old stomping grounds, Mandalay Bay. This is the sports book where I spent the majority of my time prior to moving here; the one that I would make home on weekend trips with the boys from home.

The Mandalay Bay book is a massive area that is more deep than wide. A single high wall contains a number of TVs and the bet boards. In front of it is a small area made up of rows of uncomfortable school seats with built in one-arm desks. Off to the side are rows of individual cubbies tailored to horse betting.

Up a slight set of stairs behind the rows of desks are groups of tables with 3-4 padded chairs around them. These have unobstructed views of the TVs and betting walls, while also having a small band of TVs directly in front of them. Behind them is the bar.

Arriving alone and not wanting to try to take a whole table for myself I plop down into one of the individual chairs up front. This is a huge mistake. The school seats up front are misery for anything but the shortest visit--uncomfortable and requiring you to crane your neck to watch the TVs. The higher wall of TVs and their up and down orientation means it is easier to see your game but the biggest problems are the TVs themselves. The biggest screens are projection and not HD. Until you return to watching games on non-HD screens you have no idea how important HD has become in watching sports.

So besides sitting in an uncomfortable seat, watching a poor resolution screen at an uncomfortable angle, I had to endure a guy lighting up and blowing smoke in my face. It was awesome.

In addition to betting on Northwestern at -4 in a standalone bet, I also parlayed them with Louisville, 4 point favorites against North Carolina – tying together the two teams I was most confident about to add increased profit if they both won easily as I expected.

Parlays should typically be avoided unless there is some uniting factor between the two – for example, picking a defensive oriented team to win and parlaying it with the under. Parlays are the ultimate public play –the thinking being that if you are super confident in two (or more) teams, parlay them, your outlay is less than two bets and the profit is much higher. However, there is a reason the payout is so high – they are unlikely to hit too often.

Why I parlayed these two teams, I can't say. I was extremely confident in both outcomes. In my early season naiveté I couldn't see either team not covering the spread.

The games kicked off at the same time on side-by-side TVs, giving me an opportunity to track both. In the first half, Louisville validated everything I thought; they came out and destroyed the Tar Heels like they had taken personal affront to the made-up classes many UNC players are accused of taking. By halftime, Louisville led 36-7, I was counting it as a win and I had turned my attention to Northwestern who was in a back and forth three-point contest with Boston College, trailing 13-12 at halftime.

At halftime, with a crick in my neck from looking straight up, a sore back from the uncomfortable chairs, strained eyes from deciphering the fuzzy screen and a persistent cough from the three Marlboros I was forced to inhale, I decided to move back to the table section. Forget worrying about offending a waitress by monopolizing a table, I was dying. Besides, the Wildcats needed a change in momentum.

In the second half, comfortably ensconced at a table with a cold beer in front of me, the Wildcats and Eagles continued trading field goals, and UNC woke up and started scoring on Louisiville. Here is an approximation of my reaction to each UNC score:

36-14   (How Cute! They scored!)

39-21   (Good for them! Show some pride!)

39-28   (Wait a minute…)

39-34   (Just shoot me)

After UNC got within five with four minutes to play, Louisville immediately turned the ball back over.

On the other TV, Northwestern held a 2-point lead, 15-13, and were driving for the cover clinching field goal with a couple minutes to play. I had gone from Northwestern killing the parlay to Louisville losing it in a span of two minutes.

Ultimately, on one TV, UNC faced a 4th and goal but while the Heels discussed the plan during a timeout, Northwestern running back Mike Trumpy broke a run up the middle for a touchdown and a comfortable 9-point lead on the other TV.

On that 4th down, the pass fell incomplete and the entire sports book erupted in joy (why everyone was on Northwestern and Louisville I don't know but, yes, there was a guy that ran around and high fived everyone). I had gone from digging a hole to start the day to what I would describe in text as 'a very lucrative afternoon.'

With a couple nice wins in my pocket I turned my attention to the USC/Stanford game that had kicked off during the tense moments toward the end of the Louisville and Northwestern games.

Remember that Seinfeld episode in which J. Peterman makes Elaine re-watch The English Patient after she tells him she didn't like it the first time? Sitting in the theatre while Peterman sits enraptured by a burned man lying in bed and telling stories, she is ready to commit Seppuku as a second viewing confirms her original impression.

Well, USC is apparently The English Patient of college football.

Coming off a less than inspiring win over Syracuse, I thought the Trojans would bounce back and make a statement against Stanford. Well, they did make a statement. Unfortunately for those of us betting on them that statement was 'we are really overrated.'

USC's offensive and defensive lines were dominated by Stanford. No, real championship contender can be that bad on the line. USC may rally and win the Pac-12 (as they have every other time they have fallen short of pre-season expectations in the last few years), but they can never be taken seriously as a challenger for a BCS championship berth.

I would rather sit through The English Patient again than watch an SEC team run down the Trojans' throats in the championship game.

VIKINGS (-1) AT COLTS

I am employing a new gambling system this week on the NFL. Actually, to be totally fair, I am employing A gambling system this week on the NFL. When you replace nothing with something it isn't really new, is it? Whereas previously I went with my gut and an inherent belief in things like 'always bet against a red-head QB on the road' and 'Matt Stafford will never throw three interceptions against one of the worst pass defenses in the league', I now have come up with an actual honest-to-God betting system – complete with numbers and logic and everything!

Before you laugh me out of the room (because I have nowhere else to go), I should note that this system isn't solely my work. Like all geniuses before me – Bill Gates, Mark Zuckerberg, Woody Paige – I 'leveraged' the existing work of others and re-purposed it to meet my needs. Will it work? Well, I guess we will find out.

Anyway, employing my new system betting on the Vikings came out as the best bet on the board. I take this less as endorsement of the Vikings and more an indictment of the Colts. The biggest weakness for the Vikings is pass defense – just ask Tim Tebow – but I don't think the Colts' line will be able to keep Jared Allen and company away from Andrew Luck long enough for it to matter.

On the other side of the ball, I think in his second year Christian Ponder has found a good balance that minimizes errors but allows for him to help win a game if necessary, which puts him roughly five years ahead of Alex Smith on that particular learning curve and <infinity symbol> years ahead of Tony Romo. With Adrian Peterson's remarkably quick return from ACL surgery at least keeping the Colts' defense honest, the Vikings pull out the win.

Returning to the LVH on Sunday morning for week #2, I found a quiet seat in time to watch the early game kick-offs. With my newly minted gambling system still in beta test mode after a complete overhaul following week #1, I was a little gun shy on NFL bets. With only one week of experience it is hard to say which teams are truly better or worse than expected and which just had a fluky win. Was Arizona's win over Seattle indicative of taking a big leap or taking advantage of a rookie quarterback? Did dominating wins by the Jets and Cowboys signify turning points for Mark Sanchez and Tony Romo's maturity or were they one of the four games per year where each appears competent?

The good news is that the sports book has as many questions as I do. If one actually knows the answers to those questions then there is money to be had. Unfortunately, I don't have those answers so I am keeping my bets small this week. It is a long season ahead of me. One three-team tease and one long shot money line bet with a nice payday is ultimately all I bet on.

Part of my hesitation stemmed from a distrust of the teams that my new system spit out and part of it was not having a great feel for most teams. So I hedged my bets with the tease; taking the three teams both the system and I liked the most, and teasing their spreads to give me some wiggle room in case the system ended up as buggy as the first generation of a Microsoft product. I ended up betting on a three team tease of Baltimore (+8.5) at Philadelphia, Minnesota (+5) at Indianapolis and Houston (-1) at Jacksonville.

The tease ended up being the best idea since that guy told Carly Rae Jepson he would call her, maybe. The Ravens hung tight with the Eagles, and probably should have won the game with the number of times Michael Vick handed them the ball. They fell one point short of the win but still easily covered this expanded spread (the Ravens covered the un-teased spread of +2.5 as well).

The Texans absolutely dominated the Jaguars and, moving the line down to essentially a push, meant this game was over before half-time. Sort of like the Jags' season.

The Vikings however, struggled all day against a surprisingly solid Colts defense and the predictably horrid Vikings pass defense was picked apart by Andrew Luck. However, for the second week in a row, Christian Ponder orchestrated a last minute drive for the tie that threatened to send this to overtime. Unfortunately, his heroics were undone by that poor pass defense again when Luck quickly drove the Colts into range for a game winning field goal. The Vikings lost the game, but a 3-point loss meant I covered this spread and won the tease as a whole.

My long shot bet that the Jets may actually be good this year went exactly as you would expect of a bet that hinges on 'Mark Sanchez playing well on the road.' After Saturday, I probably should have known that betting on a former USC Trojan was a bad idea.

Heart vs. Mind

Las Vegas is defined by temptation. The entire marketing campaign for the city is rooted in giving in, abandoning the caution of daily life and accepting enticements as they come. For a sports gambler there is one attraction greater than any other. It dangles out there, teasing and calling like the Sirens called Odysseus. It is a beautiful temptress, trying to suck you in only to destroy you – the lure of betting on your favorite team.

Successful gambling requires an objective, dispassionate view of the sports teams, yet most people that are drawn to sports are drawn as fans. Fans, a shortened form of the word fanatic, are not known for objectivity.

It is the great contradiction in sports betting. You are going to win the most on the teams you know best. If you have studied a team up and down, then you may have a better understanding of a team than the sports books do. In a college landscape of 120 teams, there can't be experts on every team. By focusing on a team you can gain an advantage. You can learn that team's strengths and weaknesses and understand how they match up against their opponents.

I am, and always will be, a sports fan first. I watch sports in which I have no personal rooting interest out of the pure enjoyment of competition. In a lot of ways, my favorite teams help define who I am.

Gambling or not, I will forever cheer for the Seminoles and Broncos and will live or die with their victories. But this deep love is not conducive to looking at a team and determining whether value lies in the point spread.

Betting on your favorite team is a tricky business. You can multiply the highs and multiply the lows. A win and you have doubled down on the joy of success. A loss wrecks your heart and wallet--putting you just a broken pick-up truck, and old dog away from becoming a country music song.

You can also vastly overrate your team's strengths and minimize their weaknesses. On a single weekend in Vegas, your one shot in a season to bet on your team, it is practically mandatory. A heart bet in honor of a 'Vegas, baby, Vegas' weekend with the boys is a given. But when gambling every week as a 'business' it can make any bet an even greater gamble.

Even without a bet laid on or against your favorite team, there will come a time when you are torn between cheering for your team to win and your bet to win. Especially in college football where a single loss can change a season, sometimes a game with no money bet on it can be more important than the bet of the year for a football fan.

I knew coming in that at some point I would be faced with the prospect of conflict between the business of gambling and my personal feelings, so I have spent a lot of time debating and thinking about how to handle it. Do I always blindly bet on my teams? Do I treat them as any other team and bet against them when value presents itself?

My approach instead chooses a middle ground rooted in my upbringing. If there is one thing that defines a middle-class, suburban upbringing it is avoidance. And so, I shall apply that lesson to this basic contradiction. Avoid the pain at all costs.

Ultimately, I will bet on FSU once during the entire season (outside of a very small parlay bet involving the favorite teams of my annual Vegas trip crew), and even that was a teased bet down to where they just needed to win.

For whatever reason, my emotional investment in the Broncos isn't as great as it is in FSU – in part, at least, because a single loss is less season-defining in the NFL – so I do bet on them a few times (and even bet against them once when their spread gets a little too big). I am actually able to smother my homer-instincts with an analytical hat when looking at the NFL-- however, not enough to bet on the Broncos to lose outright. If I see value on the Broncos, I bet on them. If I see value on their opponents, I avoid the game (OK, except for that one time – but trust me, it works out).

My particular perspective on this subject, though, is a little more clear-cut than it might be for others. My 'heart' teams happen to be two of the most respected and popular teams in Vegas, so it is nearly impossible to look at them and see value. In 2012, Florida State is favored by less than ten points all of once the entire season and never less than a touchdown. After a slow start in which there actually was value to be found for those more confident than I, the Broncos would become a darling of Vegas and rarely see spreads less than a touchdown. The combination of strong performance and popularity with bettors is the first paragraph in the obituary of gambling value.

With teams not only needing to win but also needing to win rather handily, it is all that much easier to resist betting on them. Do you really want to be in the conflicted position of cheering for your team to win, but also worrying about a win that doesn't cover? I know I don't.

So how do the pros handle this? Well, from what I can tell, unlike in much of sports gambling, on this particular issue there is no rule. Some pros seem to come in with no inherent loyalties that need to be shed. Maybe they went to a school without a strong football program and lived in a city without an NFL team (or just never acquired an affinity for a particular team). Maybe they aren't football fans at all, but rather pure analytics who see an opportunity for profit in sports as others see it in the stock, bond or derivatives markets.

Other pros I spoke with, while being open to 'touting' bets against their personal teams, would not bet themselves.

A third group seems to have rubbed their fandom clean over time, like sports writers who, in the process of doing their job, slowly lose the love of team that brought them to sports in the first place. When food on the dinner table requires an ability to look at teams without bias, it won't take long to prioritize your next meal over cheering for laundry as Jerry Seinfeld said.

Even in one short season, I started to notice a shift in my personal outlook. As the season went on, I lost the emotion that defined my typical annual trips. The highs and lows of bets won and lost would be replaced with a shrug of the shoulders at a bad beat or a slight smirk at a correct play. It is very easy to imagine that if this were a long term gig, the fandom in which I am cloaked would grow as thread-bare as an old t-shirt.

In the end, of the many challenges and decisions that differentiate the pros from the joes at the ticket-taking window, this may be the one hardest for an amateur to shake. Anyone with enough free time can build a quantitative system and track point-spread moves, laying bets at optimal times. But, when you are attracted to sports gambling as an out-cropping of your love of sport, it is incredibly difficult to shed that love to look at sport with a cold, analytical eye.

I write about this problem here, because, as you will see, after just a few short weeks in Las Vegas, I left town and flew to Tallahassee to watch Florida State play Clemson. While I didn't bet on FSU (they were about 13-point favorites), I still spent the weekend conflicted between my heart and my wallet.

In the days leading up to my departure I struggled to concentrate on my gambling picks, I was so consumed with the excitement of a top ten showdown returning to Tallahassee. For the first time, my bets took a back seat to my heart.

Not that I didn't lay some bets before heading across the country--of course I did. It's just that I was constantly distracted while trying to concentrate on any other game.

"Boy, I really think Syracuse could do well going into Minnesota, because FSU's defensive line can get pressure on Tahj Boyd before he can get rid of the ball."

"I know Utah had a good win over BYU, but I still think ASU can win easily because the Noles' offensive line is maturing and last week's fine running display against Wake Forest may slow Clemson's pass rush."

For me, it is all about Clemson. From their stupid orange and purple, to their germophobic nightmare of Howard's Rock to their lame booster club (IPTAY? Seriously? Not smart enough to come up with an acronym that is a word? Ok). It is ancient history that Clemson was the first college to accept me.

(Though I didn't actually apply. Seriously. They sent me an acceptance letter before I applied. Which, of the ACC schools, makes them the 'needy, sad girl we all knew in high school, totally willing to put out to anyone that says hi to her in the hall).

However, I did have a lot of fun visiting Clemson while in college, and the fraternity house we stayed in had its pledges treat my roommate and me like upper-classmen, bringing us beer and all. That was cool at the time. Now? Just the first example of Tigers sucking up to Seminoles in a desperate attempt to ensure that if we go to the Big Twelve we take them along.

Week #3

ARIZONA STATE (-7) VS UTAH

Coming off an emotional late-night win over their in-state rival and exhausted from rushing the field fourteen different times, it is easy to imagine Utah not showing up in the desert on Saturday night. Meanwhile, ASU just had a close loss at Missouri which is actually more impressive than the Sun Devils' win over Missouri last year, because Missouri is now in the SEC (it's science).

He may be the least trustworthy snake in college football not named Bobby Petrino...oh wait Bobby Petrino isn't in college football this year. Let's start over. He is the least trustworthy snake in college football but, given how well ASU is playing and how rough of a start Pitt has experienced, you can't argue with Todd Graham's work on the field.

NOTE: This pick assumes Todd Graham doesn't resign to take a new job before the game. While it obviously isn't likely, those big chicken ranching dollars have lured coaches to Arkansas mid-season before, so be warned.

NEVADA (-8) AT HAWAII

I am sure it is a totally sound philosophy to pick teams that did or nearly cost you money before, right? That is totally logical. No way this could be overshadowed by an emotional reaction. Nope. Definitely not. I am totally not basing this on the pain and stress of USF needing a last minute 50-yard bomb to beat Nevada two weeks ago. That's a crazy thought. I am just going to swallow that type of thinking right down and bury it in my gut right next to the dead carcass of the hobo from that long ago Saturday night—the evening that started with the guy at the bar asking me, "Do you know what it feels like to kill a man?"

While I want to pick Hawaii, mostly as an excuse to wave around a UH foam finger I saw in Waikiki, I just think Nevada is a sneaky good team this year with one of the leading rushers in the country. They also play at Hawaii every other year so their smart, long time head coach, Chris Ault, must have a system worked out to counteract the time zone issues.

And if Nevada fails to cover? Well, that may take me to some dark places no one wants me to go.

SOUTH CAROLINA (-10) VS MISSOURI

Missouri has played two tough home games in a row – a loss to Georgia and a close win over Arizona State. Their reward is a road trip to face the Mouth of the South (eastern Conference) and the Gamecocks. Mizzou quarterback, James Franklin , is still question-able with a painful throwing shoulder and, in any other situation, Steve Spurrier would be right now taking time away from film study to come up with some jokes to make about Franklin refusing to take painkillers. But Steve Spurrier doesn't believe in taking painkillers either. For Spurrier there is only one painkiller and it is called the Champagne of Beers.

My logic on this is simple: Mizzou lost to Georgia at home by 20 points, while still healthy and playing in front of a crazed crowd en-joying its first SEC game. You are saying they can go into a hostile environment in Columbia, banged up and licking wounds after two tough games and stay closer to a South Carolina team that is as good as or better than perennial underachieving Georgia? OOOKKK.

Maybe you should talk to Franklin about the side effects of too many drugs yourself.

FULL DISCLOSURE: I put these teams in a 3-team tease, rather than taking the lines as listed above. In my tease I got the teams at the following spreads: ASU (-.5), Nevada (-2.5) and S. Carolina (-3.5)

Over the last decade, if you wanted to make college football fans roll their eyes, tell them that you think this is the year that Florida State will return to its place among the nation's elite.

Every off-season an argument would be made for why FSU was poised to return to the pinnacle of the sport. And every year they would fall woefully short. It became the worst annual joke outside of Oregon's uniforms.

It has reached the point now that every article written this past off-season about the possibility of FSU's re-emergence were obligated to include the words 'really', 'finally' or 'we swear' in the title.

While the country has gotten a good chuckle at the annual failure of the Noles to meet lofty pre-season expectations, the impact on the Seminoles' faithful fans has been a decade of agony and frustration.

The Seminoles (and their fans) are victims of their own success. During the decade of the 1990s, the Seminoles were the dominant team in the nation: two national titles, two Heisman winners, three other championship game appearances (not to mention their annual game against Miami which on several occasions was a de facto national title game). A remarkable fourteen consecutive seasons of top-five finishes in the AP poll from 1987 to 2000. The bar that those 1990s teams set would be impossible for any team to ever duplicate. Nick Saban's Alabama team, which is now held up as the gold standard of college football, finished the 2010 season #10, so the Tide would need to finish in the top five every year between now and 2024 to equal what the Noles did.

But when the program crashed, it crashed hard. A combination of changes among and complacency within the coaching staff, more parity due to reduced scholarships and recruiting disappointments, all knocked the Noles off their perch. Since 2000 they haven't finished a single season with less than three losses.

Yet each off-season an argument is made that the alchemy of this year's team will be the magic one to bring the Noles back to the top. Noles fans spend eight months reading the stories about the talent and getting our hopes up, only to have it crushed again once the games actually start. After a solid decade of having your heart toyed with like a yo-yo, you are bound to develop some calluses. At this point a Nole fan's heart is as callused as the hands of an oil roughneck.

So you would excuse FSU fans if they approached this past weekend's game against #10 Clemson with a wary eye. A top five ranking. Dominating performances over weak opponents. The Noles were playing the 'Get Your Hopes Up Before Crushing Them' symphony to perfection.

There were some indications that this team may be different though. Fewer penalties showed a higher level of maturity than teams in the past. An absolute demolition of a Wake Forest team they had struggled to focus on in previous years. Game-breaking talent at skill positions and dominating offensive and defensive lines. It was very easy to see that this team could be different. It was easy to get excited again.

But none of that would matter if they once again failed on the big stage.

In some ways, a win over Clemson would provide neat symmetry to the failures of the Noles in this century. In 2000, the #4 ranked Noles hosted the #10 Tigers. An absolutely dominating 54-7 win propelled FSU to its last national title game appearance (almost directly, the #10 Tigers strengthened FSU's schedule enough to bump them above the Hurricanes in the BCS).

A hot, steamy afternoon was just giving way to a comfortable evening when the ball was kicked off in Doak Campbell Stadium Saturday night. The Noles had won their first three games by a combined score of 176-3, so, naturally there was hope in the crowd that the defense would dominate from the first snap. Which they did. Right up until the 5th snap, when DeAndre Hopkins broke free behind the secondary, Tahj Boyd dropped the ball in his hands and Hopkins walked in for the easy touchdown. Silence hung in the stadium from some combination of shock, disappointment and maybe just a touch of 'here we go again.'

But the FSU offense responded with their own touchdown on their first drive, notably led by the offensive line. They were dominating. Nole runners were three yards downfield before the first defenders were within a glove's reach. An optimist would have said that the offense would wear down the Tiger defenders and the Nole defense would make adjustments and slowly squeeze the Tigers like a vice. A pessimist would say something about seeing this before at Oklahoma in 2010, when each team scored on the opening drive and then OU reeled off 27 more unanswered before halftime. Unfortunately, I expect both of these were well represented in the bleachers.

The teams continued to trade scores in the first half and Clemson took a 7-point lead into halftime, 21-14. The vaunted FSU defense was barely slowing down the Clemson offense and, when they did, Clemson would find a long play to keep the drive alive. But while Clemson kept finding big plays, the FSU offense was slowly grinding the Clemson defense into pulp. Even when FSU didn't score, it was punishing the Clemson defense. The Noles second drive was 10 plays, covering 57 yards, with only 3 going more than 10 yards. But it ended in a missed field goal.

Essentially the Clemson offense was a circus - full of high wire acts, and surprising acrobatics. FSU was the tunnel grinding machine from Ocean's Thirteen – powerful, methodical and relentless. And you can imagine what one of those would do to a big top tent.

After halftime, FSU was forced to punt and Clemson responded with a trick play: receiver Sammy Watkins passed back to Hopkins for 7 points and a 2-touchdown lead. For a moment, the feeling in the stadium started slowly sliding toward resignation. Another year, another high profile disappointment.

But, blinded by a decade of pain and disappointment, the real significance of that pass went largely unnoticed. Clemson was resorting to trick plays. From that point until the last two minutes, FSU outscored the Tigers 35-3. Where Clemson was digging into chapters of their playbook that haven't seen the light of day since their offensive coordinator, Chad Morris, was in his first year coaching high school, FSU was continuing to relentlessly execute. In their next two drives, FSU scored two touchdowns in a combined five plays.

Then the defense took over. Three consecutive 3-and-outs for the Clemson offense. A rare EJ Manuel fumble was cancelled by a Nick Waisome interception two plays later. Mark Stoops had tightened the vice and Clemson quarterback Tahj Boyd's eyes were popping out of his head.

All the while, the offense's continued relentless march on the exhausted and overmatched Clemson defense may have been the real keystone that the Noles are going back to the future this season. There were no trick plays or newfangled offensive schemes to take credit for this win. There was just discipline. Quarterback, EJ Manuel, went 27-35 for 380 yards while running for 102 yards. He was poised, confident and in complete control of the Tigers, but he wasn't alone. One touchdown drive consisted of one 8-yard pass and then three runs by sophomore James Wilder, Jr. including the most physically punishing run you will see this year.

As the Noles' lead stretched to 18 points and Clemson slowly drove for a too-little-too-late touchdown with two minutes to play, the crowd's volume kept rising. It wasn't just joy at the win. It was the realization that a decade of disappointment may be nearing its end.

There are obviously a lot more games to be played and won before the Noles have accomplished anything – and if the Lost Decade has been defined by anything it has been losing games to lesser opponents through sheer lack of focus and discipline. Especially on the road.

But the team in the garnet and gold jerseys on Saturday night did not look like a group that will take a road ACC game lightly, lack discipline and make mental errors, gifting a win to a lesser team. They looked focused and determined to prove all of the jokers wrong. For the first time in a long time, the Noles served notice that they may actually be back this time. Really.

After the game it wasn't just fireworks that were released into the sky, it was the collective tension of 83,000 people that have waited twelve years for that moment.

I sure hope Oregon's uniforms are especially bad next year. They may be the only thing left to joke about.

A house divided against itself cannot stand. – A. Lincoln

I repeatedly joked about how I was struggling to focus on my gambling adventures with the looming FSU/Clemson game casting a shadow that blocked out the sun. Well, if you thought I was, I guess it's good that my gambling performance proved how true this was.

As Mr. Lincoln knew back in 1858, I was destined for a bad week of gambling and, sure enough, I ended up down on the week as a whole.

But at least FSU won. I will gladly take a small hit to the bankroll for the rest of Nole Nation.

My Saturday afternoon was spent in the hot and humid tent city on the intramural fields outside of Doak Campbell Stadium tailgating for the FSU game – drinking beer, avoiding the beergaritas and watching the potato salad turn into Patient Zero for a sequel to the movie Contagion.

Every other week, I sit in a sportsbook obsessively watching every game I have money on. And every week, the bets come down to the final minute and my ulcers grow their own ulcers. This week, I occasionally checked scores on my phone but, for the most part, didn't spend much time worrying about the games I had bet on. If FSU lost, making some money would be a hollow consolation.

So what happens this week? Does my approach mean I was able to avoid the pain of worrying over another final minute cover?

Of course not, these games were all complete blowouts.

- South Carolina 31, Missouri 10

- Arizona State 37, Utah 7

- Nevada 69, Hawaii 24

Remarkably, every game played out like I had hoped and expected. And yet I didn't get to enjoy it. No sitting back in the sports book enjoying a victory beer in the middle of the 3rd quarter. No gleeful rush to the betting window at the completion of the game to reap my rewards. Nope, instead I traded the monetary stress of gambling for the emotional stress of the FSU game. A game that ultimately ended in sweet triumph as well but certainly wasn't over as quickly as these were.

Ahh well, a win is a win is a win. And sitting down in the rapidly disassembling tailgate area in Tallahassee, a cool midnight breeze blowing, a post-victory beer scrounged from the bottom of someone's cooler numbing my worn-out throat, scrolling through scores on my phone and validating these victories was a sweet, sweet moment.

My lone Saturday loss came when the Syracuse Orange went on the road to Minnesota and played like the Big East team that they are. It is hard to imagine that the Golden Gophers actually shut down the previously explosive Orange offense, but they did, and the Gophers won 17-10. Again, I didn't watch this game, and given it was Big Ten versus Big East and was therefore undoubtedly excruciating to the eyes I am thankful for that, so I don't know how it happened--all I know is that it did happen.

Reading the recap of the game and seeing words like 'raucous crowd,' 'shutting down high-powered offense' and 'four turnovers and ten penalties,' I am extremely glad to have not sat through it.

The lesson I have learned so far this season is that if you want to bet against the Big Ten, bet against the historically good teams because they are all as lifeless as a mid-winter day in Minnesota. The historical bottom feeders – Gophers and Northwestern, Wildcats may actually be better than expected.

The Big Ten is also divided against itself, and if there is one thing that hasn't been able to stand so far this year it is my bets.

CAROLINA (-2...NO -2.5...NO -3...AHH HELL) VS NY GIANTS

This game actually opened with the Super Bowl champs as a 1.5 point favorite on the road at Carolina. But faster than a Giants player rushing to a meeting to realize Tom Coughlin's 'ten minutes early is late' mandate, the line flipped. Part of this was driven by a number of Giants' players being listed as inactive (Ahmad Bradshaw, Hakeem Nicks) and part was everyone realizing that we aren't yet in the playoffs and the Giants just haven't looked real good this year – and I'm not just referring to Eli Manning's haircut. Though that hasn't helped.

In a lot of ways Josh Freeman is just a lesser Cam Newton. He is the Sun Belt to Cam's SEC. A little slower. A little less precise. Just not quite as good, but similar. And yet Freeman went into Giants stadium, put up 243 yards and 2 touchdowns while leading his team to 34 points. Unfortunately, the Bucs also gave up 41 when Eli threw for 510 yards and 3 touchdowns and lost. The Panthers last week played the Saints - a pass-happy team with a questionable defense - at home and won relatively comfortably (by 8 after giving up a touchdown with less than 3 minutes to play) while grabbing 2 interceptions from a better quarterback in Drew Brees.

Lacking a running back, and two of his receivers (Nicks and Dominck Hixon), Eli just doesn't have the weapons to keep up with the Cam show. Really the only concern about trying to bet on this is being the last one to get money on it and getting stuck with a line of Panthers -3 or -3.5 where a field goal win gets you at best a push.

INDY (-3) VS JACKSONVILLE

If you are mathematically inclined, Jacksonville lost by 3 to the Vikings in week one. Last week Indy beat that same Vikings team by 3, so therefore the Colts are 6 points better than Jacksonville, right? Easy money.

Ok, sports is never that simple, but there are lessons to be learned from two teams playing in week three who each played the same team in weeks one and two (and in similar circumstance: Jags on the road, Colts at home). The Colts beat the Vikings by beating up on their biggest weakness (pass defense), a weakness the Jags couldn't take advantage of thanks to having quarterbacks named Blaine Gabbert (now hurt) and Chad Henne. Inversely, the Jags are at best a mediocre pass defense (17th in yardage allowed) yet in their 2nd game the Texans so dominated there was no need to even try to pass. Just because a team doesn't need to pass on you, doesn't mean you can stop the pass - one of Al Davis' lesser known Raider mottos.

Having bet on the Vikings last week, I watched the Vikings/Colts game closely and came away impressed by Andrew Luck, as well as the Colts' defense. They completely stymied Adrian Peterson (95 team rushing yards) so, I expect, they can do the same to Maurice Jones Drew, especially with the Jags having no other options on offense. At least the Vikings have Percy Harvin and Christian Ponder. The Jags have...ummm...their mascot Jaxson De Ville? And he is good for only 5-10 touches per game at most. He is soft.

In college, Thursday nights were my favorite night of the week. I'm not sure if this is the case everywhere but in Tallahassee, Thursday night was just about the biggest party night of the week – which at least partially explains how few classes were scheduled for upperclassmen on Fridays. As an athlete, Friday practices were also typically a little lighter, meaning a late Thursday night wouldn't necessarily come back up and say hello around 3:00 p.m. on Friday.

My friends and I would stop first at Bullwinkle's, where our next door neighbor poured us brutally strong $1 highballs and mocked us from behind the bar as we winced through the first burning sips. Then we would stumble up Tennessee Street to Ken's where we would sing along to David Allan Coe songs until closing time.

Re-reading that, I no longer wonder why it was a big group of guys with few women around.

Anyway, this is a long way of saying I have deeply a ingrained warm spot for Thursday nights. It is the St. Louis of weekdays: the gateway to the weekend.

But one football season in Vegas may be changing that. These weekly Thursday football games may soon become my most loathed nemesis since Steve Spurrier prowled the sidelines of the Swamp.

Twice I have confidently bet on a Thursday night NFL game. Twice I've been utterly wrong in my assessment and that game has been the precursor to a poor weekend.

I am still tinkering with the quantitative system I use to come up with my NFL picks, so my confidence was at a Brandon- Weeden-like level this week. There were games I liked that the math didn't. Vice versa—there were games the math liked, I wasn't sure about. Only one game really looked good in both ways: the Carolina game, which is why it led off my picks for the week.

Oops. Whether it was the Thursday night setting, a disrespected and hungry Giants team on the road, or the fact that the Panthers just aren't very good, this game was over by halftime Thursday night and so were most of my NFL bets.

With both the Giants' leading rusher (Ahmad Bradshaw) and one of their leading receivers (Hakeem Nicks) out, it seemed like a lock that the Panthers would win handily, which explains the line moving from Giants being favored by 1.5 to being 2.5 point underdogs. EVERYONE thought they would lose. You know, just like their last two Super Bowl appear....oh. Right.

Once again, we all got suckered by the Tom Coughlin-Eli Manning: "We aren't very good and are being overrated in Vegas" rope-a-dope. They are really becoming the Penn and Teller of dominating just when they are supposed to lose. They have been doing it for years, no one can explain how and we never really believe it until we see it.

I am done guessing which Giants team is going to show up each week: the one that can win the Super Bowl any year or the one that always needs to win in week #17, just to crack a .500 record and sneak into the playoffs.

See you in the playoffs, Tom. Don't worry, I will be ten minutes early.

As for Carolina, well, it turns out the Panthers' Superman is just a homeless dude that lives on Hollywood Boulevard and poses for pictures with tourists. The stench of Old English 800 and the handcuffs should have been a giveaway.

My only other bet was on the Colts against the Jags – a textbook case of the eye-test failing miserably.

Probably the most interesting outcome of my new life on the Vegas Strip has been the different opinions I derive by watching almost every single NFL game. Before, I would watch one or two games per week plus the red zone channel, but I am now devoting my Sunday mornings to watching every game. Whether this is a blessing or a curse, remains to be seen. But it has had an impact.

I was probably a little higher on the Cardinals earlier than most after watching them closely during their week one thumping of the Seahawks. I debated teasing them to +19.5 versus the Patriots but didn't pull the trigger. I threw them in the Tease this week but didn't bet on them outright, though I thought they had a good chance at beating Philly straight up.

I apparently was seeing the right things. Only my unwillingness to believe my own eyes has kept me from capitalizing on it (the Cardinals won but the Tease lost, thanks to the Panther epic no-show).

And so the opposite was with the Colts. Betting on the Vikings against the Colts last week I was impressed with their passing ability and defense's ability to stop the run. The 3-point spread looked too low, given the Jags' beat down at the hands of the Texans. Little did I know that the Colts' defense is fine against the run, as long as the runner isn't Maurice Jones-Drew (177 yards, 1 touchdown), who seems to dislike the Colts nearly as much as John Elway did when they drafted him.

The Colts played for a late winning (but not covering) field goal, before promptly giving up an 80-yard touchdown pass to lose the game outright.

On the bright side, since I was in the car leaving Tallahassee I didn't see the game, so I won't be talking myself into betting on the Jags this coming week.

Well, maybe....

The Number

There were many things I worried about in planning for my autumn in Vegas. Skin cancer. Emphysema. Bankruptcy; both moral and financial. Acquiring an affinity for Ed Hardy t-shirts. But one thing I didn't consider was developing a crippling case of arithmophobia – a fear of numbers.

When gambling on sports you can't avoid numbers – success and failure is quite literally defined by them. A bankroll is how you keep score; have you made money or have you lost money? A win isn't a win unless it also meets the required points. Three-team tease. Over/under line. Point Spread. Odds. Moneyline.

To paraphrase Irwin M. Fletcher, it's all numbers these days.

However, just knowing the numbers isn't enough to succeed in gambling and that's where the fear comes in. It isn't about putting money on a team to win by an amount. It is about putting money on a team to win by the right amount.

Betting on the right team at the wrong number loses just as much as betting on the wrong team. As a long time bookmaker told me, "The difference between professional gamblers and amateurs is that amateurs bet on teams while professionals bet on numbers."

It is this obsession that has gripped me and, I fear, will turn me into a mumbling lump, curled into the fetal position in a padded room before I make it out of Las Vegas.

⟩⟩⟩⟩⟩

With an established system for determining the appropriate point spread for a game, the next step is to decide whether the point spread offered demonstrates value. The best systems identify thresholds where bets make sense and where they don't. A professional bettor walks into a sports book knowing not only who they want to bet on but at what point spreads. But after that, they are at the mercy of the casino and other gamblers.

The casinos post an opening line on each game and then adjust the line as money comes in. Big money coming in on an underdog pushes the point spread down until money comes in on the favorite, reducing the casino's exposure to one side winning. Big money coming in on the favorite has the opposite impact, sending the spread up until a sort of equilibrium is once again established.

With the point spread a moving target, a Sharp has to know at what point spreads they want to buy and where they don't. They also have to be prepared to bet at a moment's notice. If the Sharp sees value in an opening line, they may need to bet big quickly, before other Sharps see the same value and the line adjusts.

This rapid response has spawned an entire sub-industry in the casino world. For a Sharp to maximize value (i.e. bet at the optimal point spread), he needs to be able to react quickly. This requires eyes on multiple casinos in real time, as lines often differ by .5-1 point between casinos based on the action they have received to date. Given the different customer types that visit different casinos, action can look vastly different on a game at different locations. A big casino on the strip will naturally attract a disproportionate number of tourist gamblers that place a bet as they stroll through the sportsbook on their way to buy another Yard of alcohol. Compared with one of the casinos off the strip, more often frequented by locals and pros, the difference in exposure for these casinos will move the point spread.

In a game where the public greatly favors a team (teams such as Green Bay, New England, Chicago, New York and Pittsburgh always receive disproportionate money) while the pros bet heavily on their opponent, the difference between a public casino and pro casino can be big. It is shopping for these differences where pros find value.

It is probably the ingrained years of business training but my mind always likens point spread shopping to the stock market. When a stock is overvalued – has risen too high relative to its underlying fundamentals, traders sell the stock if they own it or sell it short. When the stock price is too low, they buy until equal value is achieved. The same can be applied to betting on teams. If a pro calculates that New England should be favored by 7 over the Jets but they are favored by 9.5, then they are as overvalued as Pets.com in 1999. But if they are favored by 6.5, then they are undervalued. If both of these lines were available at different books, the 9.5 spread at a book where a Dunkin Donuts convention brought half of Massachusetts to Vegas for example, the pro could bet on the Jets at +9.5 at one book and then drive across town and take the Patriots at -6.5. With a perfectly accurate system he wins both bets.

This is still gambling, though, so there is no guarantee. Just as Enron manipulated their books for years and artificially inflated their own stock price, so too can a team's true value be illusory. Buying at the right price doesn't guarantee a win, but it improves the probability, which is all a Sharp is trying to do.

Obviously, the challenge in point spread shopping is knowing the spreads offered at different locations. Short of having spies at every casino or spending 24x7 driving in an endless loop up and down the Strip, it is impossible to be physically present in multiple casinos (assuming the iTransporter isn't unveiled by Apple at next year's Consumer Electronics Show). Thankfully, technology has found an answer for the well-tooled Sharp. Subscription fees ranging from a couple hundred dollars per year up to a few thousand, buys a Sharp access to constant real-time spreads at the major casinos through third party companies like DonBest. A single view desktop application or web-site gives insight into real-time spreads and vigs for every major casino chain in Las Vegas as well as statistics such as the number of bets placed on each team. Now a Sharp can sit at home (or use a mobile-phone-based equivalent), see what spreads are offered by each casino, as well as get an indication of which way the line is moving. When he sees spreads he likes he can proceed directly to the casino with the most value.

Or if they don't feel like even getting in the car, there are now mobile applications that allow them to bet through their smart phone or tablet without even leaving the couch.

Cantor and William Hill U.S. gaming have rolled out mobile betting apps so if the line moves to your liking, you can go ahead and place a bet right there from your smart phone. USC line drop to 9.5 while getting your haircut? A couple swipes on the iPhone and you can get $2,000 on that new line before you even get your neck shaved. Don't get any ideas, though. These only work in Nevada, for now.

In my nascent handicapping career, I have quickly become obsessed with the point spread. Not just the spread available but whether it is changing, which direction and when I should bet.

Unlike real pros, the system I use throughout the season focuses on relative value between different games, so I don't have a detailed approach that tells me if a line moves by .5 I should no longer bet it. For me it is more about key thresholds and which direction the number is moving.

In football gambling, there are key point spread numbers that every gambler should keep in mind and they (not coincidentally) align with the points scored on scoring plays in the game: three and seven. A large percentage of games end with point differentials of three or seven, so getting point spreads on one side of each can be a huge advantage for a casino or gambler. For a casino, the 1 point that separates a 6.5 line and a 7.5 line is much more significant than the 1 point that separates a 7.5 point line and 8.5 line. Same with the bands around 3 points (and 10 points).

With this very simple piece of knowledge, even an amateur gambler can improve their odds. Like a favorite? Try to get them at -2.5 or -6.5. Like an underdog? Aim for +3.5 and +7.5.

While DonBest offers pro gambling systems with annual fees ranging into the thousands of dollars I am too cheap and unsophisticated to sign up. Conveniently the donbest.com website also publishes a smaller subset of casino point spreads just with less information and not in real time. I may not see the moment a line changes or the Vig differences between casinos, but I do get an idea if one casino is different from others.

The two casinos that I typically visit are the MGM (attached to my condo building) and the LVH (formerly Las Vegas Hilton) where I go weekly to submit picks for the LVH Super Contest. Conveniently, donbest.com's free service publishes lines from LVH and Mirage (part of the MGM family), so I can see where the lines differ and plan my betting accordingly. I also check repeatedly and try to find the lines that maximize my chance of success.

A short example from week #1 illustrates the point of buying at the right number better than several more pages of my incoherent babbling.

One of the college games I targeted was South Florida at Nevada. USF was an underdog by somewhere between 1 and 2 points, depending on casino and day of week. I put money on USF at LVH at +1.5 while I was there because I couldn't remember what the donbest.com website said MGM was offering. Returning to the MGM that night, USF was at +2 so I put more money on the Bulls there.

In the final 30 seconds of the game, USF clung to a 1 point lead and Nevada was driving. If Nevada's drive resulted in a game-winning field goal, USF would lose by 2. I would push half of my bet (and get back that money) while losing the other half. Had I bet solely at +2, the worst I could do was push all of my money. Thankfully, in this instance the drive stalled at midfield and I cashed both tickets.

It was one small victory for me, but also a lesson in the power of numbers.

Week #4

ARIZONA STATE (+2) AT CALIFORNIA
This will mark the 3rd week in a row that I have bet on the Sun Devils. Last week they destroyed Utah at home to easily cover. The week before they lost narrowly at Missouri but would have covered for me since I had them in a 3-team tease and pushed the line down to +10 (it was a moot point thanks to another team on this list).

They seem to be consistently underrated by Vegas and I am not sure why. They have a good offense and a decent defense. They can score points. They have a young quarterback who grew up ranching in

Idaho, which means we are two wins away from someone comparing him to Jake Plummer.

Cal, on the other hand, lost at home to Nevada and the best thing on their resume was a close loss at Ohio State thanks to poor tackling on 2 long runs by Brandon Bigelow. A loss to an Ohio State team that has covered the spread once this year, which I read as 'playing down to the level of their opponents.'

I am less worried about ASU playing on the road, given they have already played well in an environment much more hostile than any-thing Cal can throw at them, now that the Tree Dwelling Protestors are gone. I am thrilled to get a couple points here and I think ASU wins outright.

Western Kentucky (-2.5) at Arkansas State

Two weeks ago the Hilltoppers tore up my Saturday evening by shock-ing the Kentucky Wildcats in overtime 32-31. I came away believing in a Hilltopper offense unafraid to move the ball on an SEC(ish) de-fense and a coach willing to trust his players to win the game rather than hope for the moral victory of a close loss.

I liked them last week as well as 3.5 point favorites over Southern Miss but didn't pull the trigger, afraid the scars of the week before were swaying me. They won 42-17. Their only loss on the season was at #1 Alabama and a combination of Hilltopper pride and Alabama indifference kept that one under the spread as well. This year the Hilltoppers are 4-0 against the spread. In the last 3 seasons they are 21-7 against the spread and 6-1 when the spread is less than 3 points (whether as favorites or underdogs).

They are also playing an Arkansas State team without one of their linebackers, suspended for the week after a cheap shot against Alcorn State last week.

I am not sure about taking a road favorite, but if any team can go on the road, it is a team that has already played in two SEC stadiums and emerged with one win.

Early Saturday morning, I went down to the MGM sports book to secure a seat for the defensive apocalypse also known as the West Virginia/Baylor game. Given the early kick-off and a chest cold I had caught in my travel to and from the Florida State/Clemson game in Tallahassee the week before, I decided not to venture out into unchartered territories and instead stuck close to home, spending the day bouncing between the MGM sports book and my condo.

Arriving at around 8:30 a.m., I ended up sitting next to an older British man in an Arsenal jersey. I made the decision to not wake up at 4:45 a.m. local time to watch the Arsenal/Chelsea game but had already confirmed that the Gunners had lost, so I asked him if he had watched. He, of course, had (in fairness, if he is still on England time that is like mid-afternoon for him), so we spent some time talking about the game and team in general while Lee Corso donned the Brutus the Buckeye head on one of the many TVs above our head. My new friend spoke quietly and with a thick working class British accent, so I struggled to follow everything he said. I would miss a few words here and there and rather than asking him to repeat himself constantly, just responded with a non-commital 'yeah' or 'ha ha' and nodded my head.

In hindsight, it was the perfect preparation for watching West Virginia and Baylor.

While I watched every play of the 70-63, 1500 yard scoring fest, I am still not totally sure exactly what happened. The things that I didn't understand, I just nodded, said 'yeah' and waited until the next score. In my memory, every single play consisted of a wide receiver streaking on a post route alone by 15 yards on his way to yet another touchdown. You will never convince me that this is wrong.

The perfect summary was a tweet by Holly Anderson, who managed the college football blog for SI.com at the time. After WVU scored a late touchdown in the first half, she posted this:

> *"Twenty-four seconds remaining on the clock. Hope the Mountaineers didn't score too quickly there."*

Two plays later, Baylor scored to tie the game at 35. At halftime.

But I was in a sports book, so while a 70-63 game was astounding to watch, it isn't the crux of the story.

The important thing to remember is that West Virginia scored 70 points in a game against a conference foe and didn't cover the point spread!

So, yes I bet on the Mountaineers and lost, but that wasn't the only thing I bet on. Thankfully, at least a few things made sense on Saturday. In fact until dusk fell on Ames, Iowa I was having a very good day.

You have to feel good about a bet when the day after you publicly call it a lock, the line moves from +2 all the way to -1.5. Such was the ride for Arizona State this week. By the time the game kicked, it had settled as a Pick, but I had locked it in earlier in the week with ASU as a 2-point underdog. Ultimately it didn't matter, because ASU jumped out to a 17-7 lead at the half and held on for a 27-17 win. While it was a nice win, I think it's only fair to pause and discuss the rather icky feeling of spending week after week supporting Todd Graham.

Graham became college football's #1 enemy after bailing on Pitt after just one season, which he had joined after four seasons at Tulsa (after bailing on Rice after one season). While he may possess the loyalty and ethics to make even Bobby Petrino cringe, there is a reason he keeps getting hired. He can coach.

I seriously doubt Las Vegas underrates his team out of some sort of moral outrage (we are talking about casinos here), but just maybe they are counting on people refusing to bet on him out of disgust. Hmm, well, if that is the case, I crossed the picket line a couple weeks ago and it has been very lucrative.

Building on the momentum of the Sun Devils' comfortable win, I captured another win when Western Kentucky beat Arkansas State 26-13 after I bet them as 2.5 point favorites. It sounds strange to say but Arkansas State was clearly overrated due to name recognition. Arkansas State this year has become like a hipster Boise State, a team to adopt early just so later one can say, "I liked Arkansas State BEFORE they crashed the BCS."

Casual fans may guess Arkansas State was a bowl opponent of Hayden Fox's Minnesota State Screaming Eagles on Coach, but people crazy (dumb, smart, addicted – choose your own adjective) enough to bet on this game know that Arkansas State is coached by Gus Malzahn, Cam Newton's offensive coordinator at Auburn (and, coincidentally, Todd Graham's Tulsa team).

With the arrival of Malzahn and a roster of players recruited by Hugh Freeze (Michael Oher's high school coach and current Ole Miss coach), Arkansas State has been a trendy team to like this season. This line actually dropped to -1.5 by Saturday.

Western Kentucky wasn't trendy pre-season but has been impressive this season. They are perfect against the spread and have lost one game – to #1 Alabama. Even as a road favorite they comfortably won 26-13.

Sometimes, this game is so easy it amazes me that Las Vegas is anything more than a Bedouin tent settlement. Between these two easy wins and the inevitable win on my three team tease of Iowa State,

Oklahoma State and Arizona State, I am going to own this place before the day is through.

Oh right, that's how they built those palaces.

Iowa State at +8.5 ultimately ended up being the weak link in my tease and lost it for me. Oklahoma State stepped up as I had hoped and battled Texas to the very end before losing on a really bad fumble non-call touchdown, but they at least covered the +8.5 spread (the expanded tease spread, not the original spread) in losing 41-36.

Iowa State, on the other hand, was in a tight battle with Texas Tech all game until the 4th quarter when Iowa State QB, Steele Jantz, turned into the worst turnover machine in the country not named Mark Sanchez. An interception turned a 1-point deficit into an 8-point deficit. A Jantz fumble resulted in a TTU field goal that moved the lead to 11. One last spread covering drive (wait…are you saying the players didn't care about covering the spread?), died with another interception so the Cyclones lost 24-13 and my tease ended up as successful as Craig James' congressional bid.

Curled up on my couch that night, relentlessly coughing up what sounded like a softball-sized glob of phlegm, wondering if I need to move to Glenwood Springs like Doc Holliday to regain normal lung function, I couldn't get too devastated by Iowa State's failure. Yes, their loss had kept me from having an exceedingly lucrative day in the sports book, but I had still come out ahead on the day. Not having any sort of system seemed to have little impact on my ability to win college football game bets.

If only West Virginia had held on for those twenty-four seconds before half, I could have had a great day.

SWIMMING WITH THE SHARPS

SAN DIEGO (+1) AT KANSAS CITY

At this point, Kansas City is just a couple years shy of being the Notre Dame "This year they are back!!" of the NFL. They had a slight improvement a couple years ago, squeaking into the playoffs out of a dreadful division but outside of that blip have been essentially DOA since the millennium. Yet, each offseason, some talking head convinces himself that the Chiefs are a dormant volcano ready to explode. And then they go out and lose their first two games by a combined 75-41 and everyone remembers (1) their quarterback didn't even start in college, (2) they are coached by Romeo Crennel and (3) their best running back almost blinded a child in the 3rd row when his ACL snapped last year.

But that is all ancient history now, because they went into New Orleans and pulled out a miracle win over a really, really sad and directionless Saints team. Sure they managed 1 touchdown on a 91-yard run but, really, this team is turning the corner.

The Chargers on the other hand looked to have finally shed that September patsy tag they have carried for the entire Norv Turner era with their wins in weeks 1 and 2. Right up until they got blasted at home by the Falcons last week.

This line just feels like it reflects too much on last week's action and not the rest of the season to date. If the Chiefs offense could barely get in the end zone against the weak Saints defense and only rank 17th despite playing from behind in every game (when defenses are softer to protect against the big play), how will they move against the Chargers' 6th ranked defense? On the other side of the ball, the Chiefs are 28th in points allowed this season. And they are favored?

After a night of being awakened by sporadic uncontrollable coughing fits, I got up on Sunday morning and returned to the LVH with more doubt in my mind than phlegm in my chest. And I have a lot of phlegm.

It is probably a bad sign that in looking for an analogy for my feelings about betting on the NFL this past week, the first thing that came to mind is Tony Romo.

Romo has been getting playing time in the NFL for the last seven seasons. Just when you start to think he has figured it out - put his wild, erratic and careless games behind him and matured into a consistent, winning quarterback, he goes out and plays like he did against the Bears. At this point, I think we need to accept that is who he is.

For every Giants game (22-29, 307 yards, 3 TDs, 1 INT, 24-17 road win), he has a Bears game (5 INTs in 34-18 home loss) or Seahawks game (23-40, 251 yards, 1 TD, 1 INT, 27-7 road loss). The only thing he has done consistently in his career is date high profile blondes. The Romo showing up for each game is a total mystery and may or may not have any relation whatsoever to the player that donned the uniform the week before.

And so it is with my NFL gambling this season. For every week one Ravens' domination, I have a Lions' no-show. For every Carolina Panthers' home meltdown against the Giants, I have a Ravens'-Vikings'-Texans' Three-team tease that cashes.

It is just hard to find any rhyme or reason to this NFL season. One week, home teams are dominating. The next, road teams rule. Favorites own one week. Underdogs win the next. Last week alone – the Chiefs won in New Orleans, San Francisco lost in Minnesota, the Falcons won in San Diego and the Cardinals beat Philadelphia.

And this week would continue my up-down, win one-lose one streak and thanks to a Romo-in-the-4th-quarter-esque desperation bet, I ended up down for the week.

Even worse, my inconsistency hasn't yet resulted in me dating Carrie Underwood.

Similar to my ASU pick in college, my bet on San Diego as a one-point underdog at Kansas City looked better and better as the line flipped from San Diego being an underdog to being a favorite. It also featured a road team playing a team getting an unrealistic amount of respect. Thankfully, the Chiefs didn't disappoint in failing to live up to expectations. The Chiefs turned over the ball five times in the first half (seven times on the game) and the game was pretty much over by halftime with the Chargers cruising to a 37-20 win.

It is hard to describe sufficiently how poorly the Chiefs played in the first half, but I'm sure they watched the Cowboys game and envied Romo's ball security.

Thankfully, I was so confident in the Chiefs' ineptitude that I doubled down on this bet, which helped offset the rest of the day.

We have all had that moment in which even as we are doing something we realize it is a bad idea. Usually these moments involve tequila. Sitting at the LVH watching football Sunday afternoon, all of my bets had expired with the morning games, but the Broncos were playing in the afternoon so I wanted to stick around and watch. Deciding I needed to liven up the proceedings I scanned the afternoon bet options and came up with a bet on the Under (23 combined points) in the first half of the Washington at Tampa game.

The logic was simple. I had watched the FSU/USF game from Raymond James Stadium the day before. A deluge shortly before kickoff had softened the field and the two teams slipped and slogged through a sloppy game with poor footing. Add in 60 minutes of football and I assumed that field would be a wreck.

Combine that with two inconsistent offenses reliant on the big play and relatively high over/under number and I decided to take a shot at making some money (I was essentially break even on the day after my first three bets).

I should have known that it was a bad idea when I approached the betting counter and, while the sheet I was looking at had the over/under number at 24, the line had moved down to 23. I should have walked away once a 14-10 halftime beat me. I should have saved my money and instead grabbed a $2 Miller Lite and a $1 hot dog and just watched the games as a fan.

Shoulda, woulda, coulda.

Of course I laid the bet. And of course both teams started slowly. Tampa scored the first points of the game with less than five minutes to play in the first quarter, and it was only a field goal. On the final play of the quarter, Robert Griffin III dove into the end zone but fumbled. It was recovered by Pierre Garcon for a touchdown. Despite being oh-so-close to getting out of the 1st quarter with only three points on the board, I was still feeling pretty good. Halfway to halftime and only ten points on the board. When a long Redskins' drive ended in a missed field goal, I thought I really might have a shot.

But that didn't last long. An interception by the Redskins was converted into a touchdown with seven and a half minutes to play. A three-and-out by the Bucs and a long run right up the middle on the ensuing Washington possession clinched the loss for me.

Sounds about right. Just when I thought things were going my way, it all came crashing down on me.

I feel you, Romo, I really do.

The Amount

With a betting system in place and a point spread we like, we are all set to beat the casinos; to win so much that Steve Wynn comes crawling to us asking for a loan.

But how much to bet? In theory, if the system works and the number is optimized we should be willing to bet the mortgage. In theory.

In theory, David Tyree could never make a catch using one hand and his helmet while Rodney Harrison's HGH-fueled-arm tomahawk chopped at him.

The football field is where theory goes to die. So, making the right decision on how confident you are on a bet is the difference between starring in a movie that ends with your arm around a super model as the camera pulls back from your palatial mansion and a 2-minute mid-film montage that ends with mobsters breaking your arm.

No one always beats the house (a 60% win rate would make you a legend) so it's important to take advantage when you do see an advantage. Maximize your best bets and hope you do well enough on other bets to not lose all of your winnings.

The single most important decision to make is the amount of your total bankroll. How much are you willing to lose over the course of the season (or weekend, or year; whatever time period you are planning)? It should be enough that you can place the bets you want to make but not so much that, if you lose it all, your best option left is to just walk out into the Nevada desert like an elderly Inuit climbing onto an iceberg and floating out to sea.

Besides the amount, it is critical to acknowledge the difference between a gambling bankroll and a savings account. Over lunch with Jimmy Vaccaro, one of the most legendary bookmakers in Las Vegas, we discussed this very concept. When a man who has been in Las Vegas since 1975 (and was gambling for twenty-five years before that) gives you advice on gambling, it pays to listen.

As Jimmy noted, it is absolutely critical to differentiate a bankroll from the money used for everyday expenses. Everyone – every pro, every amateur, everyone – will hit a cold streak. If your bankroll pays your monthly rent, what exactly will pay the rent the month you lose money? Counting on consistent big wins to directly support your life is the fastest way to go broke gambling. In the end you absolutely need two pools of money – one for living expenses and one for gambling.

Once the total bankroll is defined, then the next step is determining how much to lay on any single game. There are various schools of thought on betting amounts but the simplest and most straightforward from my point of view is to develop a unit based system.

The best way to approach this is to put the two end stakes in the ground. If a game just squeaks through the system by the barest amount and you decide to bet, what is a number you are comfortable betting – the amount you would put on your least confident games.

Then flip the script. What is the amount you would bet on a game that you feel is as close to a sure thing as can be found in Clark County. A game that fills you with so much confidence it is as if Tim Donaghy was refereeing the game and whispered in your ear, "Don't' worry, I got this."

However, one word of caution when gambling for the long haul. Weird things happen. The max on any single game shouldn't be your entire bankroll. Those gambling for the long haul typically suggest a max bet of no more than five to ten percent of your bankroll.

You now have a minimum and maximum bet. This is your betting range, so next you can create tiers within that range, maybe up to five tiers. Based on your confidence level for a game coming out of your system and the numbers available, you can slot each bet into one of those tiers.

I will note two exceptions to the tiering approach. Fun or emotional bets probably should be smaller than a tier one bet. Betting on the alma maters of every family member may be fun since you are cheering for them anyway, but it is no way to make a living. Though, admittedly, the McIntire family teaser has performed admirably for me in the past.

On the other side, if Tim Donaghy really is refereeing a game and whispers in your ear, "Don't' worry, I got this," I would bet everything I could find, including my parent's china. But that's just me.

As for my adventure this year, here is my actual approach. Though a word of caution - I am not a millionaire, nor am I backed by a big money syndicate. I am just a guy lucky enough to have built up some savings and investments that I could tap to live six months with essentially no income outside of winning at gambling and the odd freelance writing gig.

My bankroll is $10,000. That is how much I am willing to lose and when creating my budget for these six months, the amount I assumed

I would lose. If you divide it across twenty weeks of NFL, that is roughly $500 per week to bet. That is small potatoes and I know there are casual bettors that spend my entire bankroll on one lazy Sunday in the sports book. Fine, I get it. But remember you may spend that in a weekend. I have to survive twenty weekends (plus college bowl games).

Also, it is important to differentiate bankroll and bets laid. A bankroll doesn't constitute the total amount bet but rather the total amount that a bettor is willing to lose. Even the most casual gambler will win occasionally, so the bankroll is the worst case scenario, not an arbitrary cap on bets laid. For my experiment, I ultimately will lay bets totaling closer to $20,000, and never really endanger wiping out my entire bankroll.

To get a sense of whether I could really live as a gambler based solely on winnings, the easiest thing to do would be to add a zero or two to each number you see in this book. If I bet $100 – a tier two bet for me – a pro would bet either $1,000 or $10,000. Simple math tells you this would require a bankroll of $100,000 or $1 million.

It also gives you some idea regarding the amount of money needed to make a living at this. A bettor needs to win 52.4% of equal sized bets to break even (thanks to the vig). The ceiling for a bettor is typically assumed to be around 60% win rate. Some quick math and it is easy to see that even a large bankroll won't net a huge profit when losing 40% of the bets over time. One million dollars in equal sized bets with a 60% winning percentage, results in a $145,000 profit; a nice living but given that the at-risk amount was $1 million, not a great income relative to the risk.

It also drives home the need to tier bets based on confidence. If a bettor wins the big bets and loses the small bets, the win rate becomes less relevant to his total take home.

In the end the lesson is the same. Whether it is winning $45 on a bet or $4500, are you winning more than you are losing? Are you winning enough to live and continue betting?

As for my tiering system, at least initially, I am starting at $50 and scaling up to $250. Five tiers of bets.

At least initially. Admittedly, with months of gambling in front of me (and years of fiscally conservative upbringing behind me) I am overly cautious early in the season.

It is the great paradox. Over time, as I am still getting comfortable both with my own ability and the teams on which I am betting, so too are the books getting better with lines. Value dries up a little more each week. My conservative nature misses out on chances to win big money. In short, I don't have the cojones to truly be a gambling pro.

A perfect example of the conundrum I face happens in week #4. The Chargers are visiting the Chiefs. From all indications, the Chiefs are not good, but pulled out a miracle win at the struggling Saints the prior week. After an uncharacteristically strong start the Chargers got crushed at home in week #3 by the Falcons. The Chargers open as a 1-point underdog. Both the logic from watching both teams and the numbers in my nascent system scream that this is a horrible line. It seems to imply Vegas is thinking 'here we go again' on another bad start of season for Norv Turner and San Diego and that the Chiefs are better than they showed in the first couple weeks.

I couldn't disagree more strongly. My system said the Chargers are demonstrably better than the Chiefs. I was completely confident the Chargers would dominate. But I didn't trust myself and enough doubt sat deep in my overly analytical brain that I wimped out. I labeled it a Tier 2 game and bet $100.

The Chargers won 37-20 and the outcome was never seriously in doubt from the end of the first quarter.

Steve Fezzik summed up the issue nicely in an interview with StatFox in 2009.

Fezzik said, "This is one of my pet peeves, since all the experts say to start slow. In my opinion, that is terrible advice. The very best wagers are made in May for the upcoming football season. The people that do their homework early and quickly, make bets like Broncos and Bengals as Pick (now Bengals -3), which is just a sick bet. That doesn't guarantee a win, but you won't find a better play for a variety of reasons… Earlier in the year, the numbers are much further off than later in the year. For those waiting for perfect information, comes perfect lines or very tight lines. Your largest wagers should come early in the year, if you are prepared. And I don't know any professional gambler that would disagree with that."

However, for new gamblers, in the same article, Fezzik says: "I would simulate the first 200 bets and track how you are doing before betting. Keep track if you are winning or losing and write down why you would have made the bet. Next if you want to bet, I would bet peanuts; way less than you think you should bet."

So take advantage of the bad lines by betting early…but keep your bets small until you are more comfortable…but the value is gone.

For the record, in the Bengals/Broncos game referenced by Fezzik above, the Bengals led all game until the final seconds, when a ball was batted by a Bengal defender to Brandon Stokely, who ran it in for a game winning touchdown.

But getting Bengals as a Pick was a nice bet. In theory.

Week #5

UCLA (-2) AT CAL

Last week, my favorite bet was taking Arizona State going into Cal. The logic was simple. Cal stinks. Arizona State is pretty good. ASU was an underdog, but outside of a 2-4 point swing what is the difference between last week and this week?

UCLA is pretty good. They won on the road last week (though it was at Colorado, so bragging about that road win is sort of like taking a long weekend ski vacation on the blue slopes at Breckenridge and claiming you once filmed a Warren Miller movie) and dominated a decent Nebraska team at home.

I use 'decent' here as - per NCAA regulations - it is the most positive adjective that can be used to describe a Big Ten team this year.

I don't understand Vegas' continued fascination with Cal. What have they shown to make anyone think they are within a couple points of any Pac12 team not located in Boulder or Pullman?

Oh well, as long as Vegas remains as suckered by Jeff Tedford as the Cal administration, I am fine with it. Keep it up all season and I may make so much money betting against Cal, I will be able to afford to buy Tedford's house. Irony!

MARSHALL (+3 - EVEN) VS TULSA

My approach to picking games this season has been driven by two approaches – the football and the spread.

Think of it like stock market day traders. Some guys buy and sell stocks based on the underlying value of the company – new products, cost-cutting initiatives and high earnings are the drivers of value.

Other guys buy stock based solely on the momentum of the market. Economic questions? Invest in gold, because when economic questions fly, money looks for safe value and nothing is safer than gold. Doesn't matter if a company is well run, if it is in the right place at the right time, momentum can drive stock prices higher. Alternatively, no matter the underlying fundamentals, if the market dislikes a company, that company is dead. Just ask Lehman Brothers.

UCLA v Cal is a football pick. I just think UCLA is better than Cal. And more than two points better than Cal.

Marshall on the other hand is a spread pick. I like Marshall's high-flying offense and I like them at home but this comes down to performance in a sports book not on the field. Marshall has covered three straight spreads, including on the road at Purdue last week. Tulsa has failed to cover a spread the last two weeks, playing closer than expected games against Fresno State and at UAB. They have also yet to cover the spread on the road at all this season.

Whether this wins or not, I feel so cutting edge using this approach that I am going to roll over these winnings into a multi-screen set up and a headset to yell my bets at the sports book manager.

Actually worrying about the football teams playing is SOOO 1990s.

The year 2012 has been the butt of more jokes than any year since 1984. With the apocryphal story of the Mayans picking the end of the world for December, Armageddon and 2012 have become as synonymous as firing Big Bird and misunderstanding the national deficit.

While the Mayans may have projected the apocalypse for December, for me it arrived a little early.

Specifically on Saturday.

I knew going into this little experiment that not every day would be Christmas. I would take the good and take the bad. I would take them both and there I would have the facts of life in Vegas. They don't build these palaces in the desert by making gambling easy.

However, I did not expect for everything to go cataclysmically wrong to such an extent that it would bleed over to my (non-bet upon) favorite college football team and even my baseball team.

That is when Saturday went beyond a bad betting day. In the grand scheme of things I didn't lose a ton of money. Yes, I lost all but one small bet, specifically placed as a hedge to a hoped-for bigger payday, but that would have been ok. It was the combination of my heart team losing to become (or should I say 'returning to') a national punchline, on top of a day of missed opportunities and lost bets that made this day feel like rocks were raining from the sky and fire flowed through the streets.

Ok, maybe I am exaggerating slightly.

The day started positively. I sat in my sun-drenched condo while I drank coffee, polished off College GameDay and started to watch the early morning games. I had placed both a parlay and a tease bet on Arkansas to pull the upset over Auburn so I cheered on the Razorbacks and sure enough they dominated the Eagles, winning 24-7. The day was off to a fine start when I decided to head down to the MGM sports book for the mid-day games. I wanted to watch the Marshall game as well as the Florida/LSU game. I teased Florida with Arkansas and Missouri, based on a belief that even if they couldn't actually beat LSU, the Tigers' offense wasn't capable of winning by a large enough amount to beat the teased spread (+9.5). Sure enough, not only did the Gators keep it close, they (unfortunately for an FSU alum) won outright, 14-6.

On another screen, a back and forth game came down to Marshall in the Tulsa red zone twice late in the second half needing a touchdown to tie the game. After some abysmal play calling which consisted entirely of runs up the middle, short passes to nowhere and long passes to the end zone on 4th down – because 'let's not worry about just picking up the first down, let's keep going for it all' (really, I'm not bitter), the Herd failed twice to score and lost by seven, 45-38.

At the time I shook it off as a price of doing business – one of the inevitable losses where my team ultimately fell short in the end, a momentary blip on an otherwise successful day, so far.... I still had the UCLA/Cal game, a tease alive and a parlay of Arkansas and Miami to pull a big upset on Notre Dame. I still had a good chance to end up having a successful day.

As the sun began to set I was back in my condo watching the Florida State game at North Carolina State on one TV, the Miami-Notre Dame game on another and the Missouri-Vanderbilt game online (a bet on Missouri -.5 was the final leg of a three-team tease with Arkansas and Florida).

It is not often that two game-changing plays occur on the first drive of a game but in the Miami-Notre Dame game, they did. On the first drive, a Miami wide receiver dropped two separate long touchdown passes after getting behind the Notre Dame defense; a missed chance to put the Irish on their heels and suck the air out of a partisan crowd in Chicago. Notre Dame's offense started moving on the Miami defense in long sustained drives and slowly pulled away after the Hurricane offense could get nothing else going. A 13-3 halftime deficit ballooned to 34-3 in the 3rd quarter and the Canes were done.

On my main TV, Florida State was dominating the Wolfpack but repeatedly stalled out in the red zone, mostly settling for field goals instead of touchdowns, taking a 16-0 halftime lead. But the defense was dominating and it was hard to imagine NC State sustaining a drive for a touchdown. Even just 16 points seemed relatively safe.

On my computer, Missouri was in a tight game with Vanderbilt, a team whose only win to date this season was over something called Presbyterian. Missouri suspended five players before the game due to a mid-week drug bust (after I laid the bet, of course) but still led early and were dominating a bad Vanderbilt offense.

However Mizzou lost starting quarterback, James Franklin, to a sprained knee in the first quarter, misplayed snaps cost them a safety and an extra point, and they slowly relinquished the early lead. They never could mount a comeback behind their backup quarterback, losing 19-15. In hindsight, it probably wasn't smart to bet against any school that wins a football game against an entire religion.

After halftime of the FSU game, I had to leave. Having already written off Miami and Missouri, my only chance at profit sat on UCLA's shoulders. As I walked out the door, the 2nd half of the FSU game started similar to the first half with the disconcerting development that NC State was starting to show a little life on offense.

Quite randomly, the Nuggets played a tip-off preseason game against the Clippers at Mandalay Bay. Since missing the majority of the Nuggets' season this year after owning season tickets last year, I decided I couldn't pass up my one chance to watch the boys, so I pulled myself away from the Seminole game early in the 2nd half and wound my way to the Mandalay Bay events center.

It was a Clippers home game, so I was one of the few in baby blue among a surprisingly vocal Clippers fan base. I mean, it was a meaningless preseason game but these fans acted like it was the Western Conference Finals. I guess being the ignored little brother of NBA basketball in L.A. will make you desperate.

Only partially watching the game, I was getting constant text up-dates on the FSU game. After I had departed, NC State put together a couple drives and trailed 16-10 late in the 4th quarter, with one last drive to try and win the game. Remarkably converting two separate 4th downs, the Wolfpack made it inside FSU' ten yard line with less than a minute to play. The writing was on the wall. When NC State scored the final touchdown on yet another 4th down play to clinch the FSU loss, I stuck my phone in my pocket and didn't look at it again. I tried to enjoy the Nuggets game; to enjoy the little cocoon I spun to keep myself from the rest of the world laughing at FSU's failure.

Before turning off my phone, I got one last text saying 'UCLA is los-ing 16-7.' I just replied, 'Well, of course they are.' When I stopped by the Mandalay Bay sports book to cash an old ticket, I noticed UCLA trailing 36-17 (they would give up one last touchdown and lose 43-17) and it actually gave me sort of a perverse thrill. I mean, a loss is a loss. If you are going to lose, then go down hard. Don't pretend and fight and give your backers hope. As the Expendables franchise has proven: the bigger the boom, the better the train wreck.

After the Nuggets game (won by the Nuggets on a Ty Lawson lay-up at the buzzer – making them the only one of my teams to win a game on Saturday and it was meaningless), still unable to imagine turning on television, I broke my seal and hit the blackjack tables.

One thing I hadn't considered in planning this trip is how all-encom-passing football would become in my life. My only sense not being bombarded 24x7 by football is taste. I read the internet, watch TV, listen to podcasts, type on my laptop, carry betting sheets and smell the cigarette-smoke-scented air of a sportsbook pretty much every day. In many ways it is a dream and what I wanted when I left my other job and decided to do this – to actually focus on football, not as an afterthought, but as a vocation. However, on a night like Saturday

- when every highlight or comment is an acupuncture needle jabbed in a little too far - it is torture.

I wanted – no needed - to forget about sports and guzzle vodka-sodas for a while. I wanted the time-warp that comes with sitting at a table in a casino. I wanted the dull haze that settles in your brain with multiple drinks and doesn't really hit you until you stand up and try to walk away. I wanted to be numb for a bit.

This is most certainly not a Dr. Oz approved way of dealing with disappointment but I wanted to hit rock bottom to start the long climb back.

I sat down at a table in MGM somewhere around 10:00 p.m. Moments later, my first drink arrived; shortly thereafter so did my first blackjack.

Four and a half hours and at least seven...or maybe eight...drinks later, I stood up a couple hundred dollars lighter, said goodnight to new friends from Toronto and Minnesota that I will never see again and stumbled back to my condo.

The next morning, I finally roused myself a little after 10:00 a.m. The sun was streaming through my curtains and NFL games were already playing. It was a new day and I had more money at stake.

The apocalypse had come and gone yet I am still here.

The Mayans were full of it.

MINNESOTA (-5.5) VS TENNESSEE
Minnesota has been one of the surprises of the season, jumping out to a 3-1 record with wins against the Forty-Niners and at Detroit last week. Adrian Peterson has looked solid if not spectacular coming off a torn ACL, quarterback Christian Ponder has looked mature and

minimized mistakes. The defense still has a bad secondary but its pass rush has helped minimize the damage inflicted.

Tennessee on the other hand has started out as lethargic as a frat kid after a night of vodka enemas. Chris Johnson is running as well as he spells on Twitter and quarterback Jake Locker is hurt, being replaced by Matt Hasselbeck who was a fine quarterback back in 2005. Of course, so was Matt Leinart. If the athletic Locker got hurt behind this offensive line, Hasselbeck may need to retire at the half. Vikings at home look like a lock from here.

CHICAGO (-4.5) AT JACKSONVILLE

Coming off a big Monday night win in Dallas in which their quarter-back wasn't the one throwing more passes to the opponent than his own teammates, finally, the Bears are riding high and looking to come in and dominate a lowly Jags team. With Jay Cutler taking care of the ball and not chewing out his teammates, the Bears should be able to move the ball well on a Jags defense ranked 26th in yards allowed.

On the other side of the ball, a Bears defense ranked #3 in rushing yards allowed should be able to shut down Maurice Jones-Drew and put the ball in Blaine Gabbert's hands. If Tony Romo turned the ball over five times against this defense, Gabbert may end up throwing ALL the interceptions. If there is no Monday night hangover, the Bears should cruise.

Several years ago, I had a client that was originally from Turkey. He was about my age with thinning hair, glasses, a goofy smile and a thick accent. He was a nice guy and I got along well with him – to the point he (half jokingly) told my boss he wanted to hire me and told me if I ever went to Turkey I would be welcome at the seaside resort run by his parents. But his general friendliness isn't why I bring him up – nor do I have a pending trip to Turkey planned. It was a more profound effect he had on my life. He was the wisest sports philosopher I have ever met. Yet, he probably didn't know it. He wasn't a big sports fan but he taught me one of the most fundamental lessons I have ever learned as a sports fan. A lesson I think about or quote literally once every week or two.

One day, sitting in his small office, I lamented something about the poor performance of one of my teams over the weekend (most likely FSU). He just smiled and said:

"Well, you know, God is an accountant. Every debit needs an off-setting credit."

It has been said in many different ways – "what goes around, comes around," "it is always darkest before the dawn," "every action has an equal and opposite reaction," "when a girl walks in with an itty bitty waist and a round thing in your face, you get sprung"…wait, no, that last one is something else – but it makes it no less true.

"God as accountant" is a simple concept – but then most wisdom is. And yet it is also remarkably true. Holding this in the back of your mind keeps you grounded when things are going well and helps lift spirits when things are dark.

And so after an abysmal Saturday when absolutely nothing went right for me, I should've expected a rebound on Sunday. I should have known that things would turn out better.

With 3 points for home field advantage, the point spread implied that Minnesota was only 2.5 points better than Tennessee, which is absurd. The 4-1 Vikings have been one of the biggest surprise teams of the season so far and it is clear Vegas has not bought in. The Vikings have won on last second drives, special teams plays and by totally dominating the best team in the league, yet every game seems to have come with an asterisk. Wait, why I am complaining about this?

So, yeah, Vegas: the Vikings TOTALLY stink and are getting lucky with these wins.

The Titans on the other hand are just not good. A running back that plays like a gallon of milk that expired in August. No wide receiving talent. A sieve of a defense. Forced to start a back-up quarterback only marginally younger than the state of Tennessee. Why anyone thought they could hang with the Vikings in Minnesota when the 49ers had gotten thumped there two weeks prior made no sense. It always seems easier in hindsight but I can't understand how anyone could not see the Vikings 30-7 win coming.

Not that I am complaining. In fact, I think this win was fluky too. I think the Vikings should be underdogs to the Redskins and their back-up quarterback this week. Big underdogs. Like double digits. Come on Vegas, don't let them fool you.

Thankfully the Vikings weren't the only validation I had to my opinions, though. I don't have a lot of deeply held gambling beliefs, but I do have one. If I can get three clearly superior teams with lines where they just have to find a way to win, such as Baltimore at Kansas City, Atlanta at Washington and Chicago at Jacksonville I will take it.

The system I am using to help guide my NFL picks consistently overrates superior road teams. Looking at just the difference between two teams and the line, it spits out small road favorites as the best bets on the board each week. I am still adjusting to try and reduce this effect but there is one way to do it – put them in a tease. Baltimore's anemic performance in Kansas City failed to cover the spread (-5 or -6) but by teasing them I brought them down to just needing to win – which is pretty much all they did, out-dueling Kansas City in a field goal contest 9-6.

Atlanta and Chicago on the other hand both turned in professional wins in road games against lesser teams. They turned in performances that show maturity and confidence – something often lacking when teams hit the road in the NFL (see: Green Bay Packers vs Indianapolis Colts).

My system isn't perfect – by no stretch. But each week it gets better and the careful use of a tease to help smooth out the rough edges of its predictions can help save it from itself.

That, and God owing you one.

The Contest

(Adapted from an article that appeared on SBNation Longform in November 2012)

As the sun descends behind the Spring Mountains a steady stream of taxis carry tired vacationers from the Las Vegas strip to McCarron Airport. Further out in the endless sprawling sub-divisions ringing the city, families prepare for a return to work and school the next morning.

On the sports book floor of the LVH Hotel and Casino, as the afternoon NFL games come to an end, cheers and groans are replaced by a low hum as bettors fortunate enough to have a ticket still worth more than the paper it is printed on form lines at the betting windows.

Jay Kornegay, however, sees none of it. The Vice President of Race and Sports Book Operations at the LVH (formerly Las Vegas Hilton) is in his office.

Back here, down a winding overstuffed hallway behind the sports betting windows, things are much quieter. The hardest part of the week is just about over. Sunday is the peak of every week for the LVH and Kornegay. With Football Central projecting all of the NFL games and another week of the LVH's handicapping competition, the SuperContest, wrapping up, Sunday nights here are what Friday nights are for the rest of the world.

Kornegay's office is located past the break room, past the bulletin board and mail boxes , and after a right turn where there is a large computer room with the glass walls to the left. The computer room looks like it might be a part of NORAD, but instead of Air Force officers tracking Russian ICBMs, the seats are filled with young analysts monitoring where money is flowing and adjusting the betting lines accordingly.

Jay's office doesn't look like that of a NORAD commander. It is more like a high school principal's office with a wall of security monitors tracking the movements of students. But here the TVs are turned to every sporting event being played. The other walls show that, despite being in the business of sports, Kornegay is first a fan, particularly of the Denver Broncos.

All that is left at this point is for Jay to review next week's point spreads one more time. He makes minor adjustments based on what has transpired on fields across the country and looks for weakness based on where the bettors are sending their money. When it comes to the accuracy of point spreads, the market efficiency with which bad lines are attacked and adjusted would make Alan Greenspan's heart sing.

After that final task is done, Jay may make it home in time to watch the second half of the Sunday night game like any other football fan. Jay isn't much of a gambler himself, and is not allowed to bet at the LVH, so when away from the office he watches a game as a fan rather than a gambling professional.

⌇⌇⌇⌇

If it had been solely up to Jay Kornegay, he never would have even come to Las Vegas. Out-voted 7-1 by his friends at Colorado State University, Jay first visited Las Vegas in 1987 for spring break in his senior year. After surviving the Vegas baptism of trying to place a bet using the team name rather than the designated bet number – a common mistake every novice makes - Kornegay became intrigued by the idea of working in the gaming industry. He convinced his then-girlfriend to move to Reno and give casino life a try. After a few years, they were able to transfer to Las Vegas and a life path was set. That path ultimately led him to the LVH.

In person, Kornegay is the antithesis of the casino boss pictured after too many hours spent at the movies. He isn't a hulking man with slicked-back hair wearing an Italian suit, cracking the kneecaps of a debtor. Small and wiry with short cropped, dark, thinning hair and matching goatee, when he greets the attendees of Football Central on Sunday he is usually wearing a Bronco jersey. On weekdays, working in his office behind the sports book, he prefers business casual.

With a reputation for being friendly, trustworthy, and offering innovative bets, Kornegay and the LVH have built a sterling reputation among the "wise guys" – the big bettors that keep the Las Vegas casinos humming in between the bachelor parties and March Madness..

Every casino on the Las Vegas strip loves NFL Sundays. Every sports book is packed with people throwing money on their favorite teams or a team that looks like they might be a good deal before kick-off. But no casino lives for NFL Sundays quite like the LVH.

One block removed from the Strip and nearly eclipsed by the luxury hotels that have sprouted up along it, the LVH has nevertheless built a reputation as a Las Vegas destination because of its sports book. Beyond a broader array of bets available than many other books, LVH has also developed NFL-centric offerings that cater to casual and serious bettors. There is Football Central, the dedicated theater showing only NFL games on eleven HD screens.

Then there is LVH's NFL SuperContest. A year-long handicapping competition open to anyone willing to put down $1,500 and find a way to submit their picks each week in the LVH sports book. In recent years the SuperContest has grown at a rate that a decade ago seemed unimaginable.

As Kornegay explains it to me, the Super Contest was started in 1989. Possibly. Maybe 1988. But definitely sometime in the late 1980s. Between changes in ownership and management at the LVH, and the vast number of concerns of a functioning sports book – juggling all of the daily games, horse races as well as futures bets in a pre-internet world -- the historical documentation of a small handicapping contest among a few locals and pros has never been a priority. As a result, much of the early history of the SuperContest is hazy at best. That seems appropriate. Aren't most of our initial memories of Las Vegas a little fuzzy?

The basic idea was simple and remains so to this day. Bettors put down $1,500 at the beginning of the NFL season and each week the casino posts contest-specific, static point spreads for each game. Then, before a specific deadline, bettors come to the LVH and pick five games against the spread. The participant with the highest number of correct entries at the end of the season wins. The contest reduces gambling to its core: the bettor with the most correct picks wins.

Already a popular destination for wise guys, the SuperContest initially attracted a devoted following through the enticement of a payout in the low six figures and a high profile victory against the sharpest bettors in town. As the contest has grown, participants have remained enthusiastic over the ever growing payout but just as significantly, over the prestige that accompanies a victory. Prestige that can, quite literally, define a career.

Initially, part of the value of the SuperContest to the Las Vegas Hilton went beyond any profit from the contest itself. The idea was that a kind of an "Algonquin Round Table" of wise guys would show up every Friday night to submit their Super Contest picks. Not only would they bet, but their presence would also attract other bettors curious to see which teams the wise guys liked that week. The SuperContest was the chum to start the feeding frenzy each Friday night; the real prize wasn't necessarily the sharks but the scavenger fish fighting over scraps and dreaming of becoming sharks themselves.

By 1999, the SuperContest had grown to 257 participants. The winner, Russ Culver, took home $154,200 out of a total purse of nearly $350,000. Other casinos started similar contests but none ever achieved the steady growth and popularity of the more established SuperContest. Despite its success – or perhaps because of it -- contestants remained almost exclusively either professional sports gamblers or Las Vegas-based amateur bettors who still worked a day job. By law, participants had to place their bets in person, which tended to keep the contest local.

In 2005, the year after Kornegay joined the LVH, the contest attracted a record 505 entrants. While still dominated by 702-area code locals, an influx of new entrants from out of state began to fuel the contests growth. As Kornegay describes it, "It was a good mix of pros and wannabe pros. Not that many Average Joes out there. It was mostly pros to semi-pros, and then you had a little mix of Average Joes." As a result, an entire cottage industry popped up to support this trend. 'Proxies' -- people that, for a nominal fee, deliver the betting card to the betting windows so entrants don't need to be in town -- started to have an impact.

꜀꜀꜀

While Jay haunts the back corridors at the LVH, Dave Tuley sits quietly in his corner office also finishing up his work day.

Occupying the front row, corner seat in the VIP-only balcony of Football Central, Tuley has spent the day watching football. As he does he takes notes on his small Acer laptop and posts them in real time in the forums of his gambling information web site ViewFromVegas. com. After he completes his final comments on the afternoon's games -- who won, who lost and who covered the point spread -- he too will pack up his computer and head home.

In addition to tracking all of the football action with a Vegas-trained eye on point spreads and over/under lines, Tuley will note how the games played out for the most common selections among LVH SuperContest participants. While not officially associated with the contest, Kornegay refers to him as "The Gatekeeper," the SuperContest's de facto historian and documentarian. His day isn't quite as close to complete as Kornegay's though. After he gets home he will still need to monitor and report on the Sunday night football game and begin the task of handicapping and prepping for next week's action.

Since moving to Las Vegas in 1998, Tuley has become a walking encyclopedia of Las Vegas gaming, in particular handicapping contests. Possessing a round, open face and friendly disposition, he comes across more like a small town accountant or doctor than a gaming journalist. Since the late 1990s, Tuley has held a front row seat to the growth of the LVH SuperContest, covering the event each year in the same way a football beat writer covers a team.

A victim of the recession (and recessionary print media industry), in 2007 Tuley was let go from the Daily Racing Form. He then started ViewFromVegas.com, reporting on the happenings in the world of sports as seen through the prism of a betting window. This led to freelance work including writing a weekly column for the Las Vegas Review-Journal, ESPN.com and back with The Daily Racing Form.

By approaching the handicapping contests in the late 1990s with a journalistic view first, rather than strictly as a handicapper, Tuley has achieved a unique position from which to witness the growth of the LVH SuperContest while still maintaining a reputation for objectivity. He doesn't sell gambling tips (i.e. act as a 'tout') and doesn't write for pick-selling websites. Tuley, though, does remove his hat of neutrality long enough to also be a participant in the contest, and he can handicap as well.– He went 5-0 in the SuperContest Week Six this year, which propelled him into the Top Five in the overall standings, validating a 14th place finish in 2008 – but his primary focus remains reporting. He was one of the first people to recognize the value in the distribution of SuperContest information, which increased interest in the competition. Yet he also monitors, reports and participates in contests held by other casinos, and sees how and where the SuperContest differs from its competitors. As much as anyone, he has seen where the contest has come from and where it might go.

❧❧❧

After the 2005 SuperContest set a record with 505 entrants, the economic downturn caused a drop in participation. Yet at the same time the visibility of the SuperContest grew. First, local pro, Steve Fezzik, won back to back contests in 2008 and 2009, attracting media attention. Then Chad Millman, Editor-in-Chief of ESPN the Magazine and ESPN sports writer, Bill Simmons began participating in the contest and openly discussing their individual picks and standings, both online and in podcasts on a weekly basis.

What was once a little-known contest for a handful of professional gamblers began to be discussed and monitored across the country by not just gamblers but by football fans. The recent rise of social media, especially Twitter, has compounded the phenomenon. The mass intimacy of social media has turned the SuperContest into a spectator sport.

Consequently, as the economy has recovered, participation has grown. In 2011, a record 517 entrants signed up. The LVH was so caught off-guard by the unexpected growth that they even ran out of the T-shirts they give to participants. This makes the 2011 LVH SuperContest T-shirt not just a $1,500 T-shirt, but a limited edition $1,500 T-shirt.

ᴊᴊᴊᴸ

While Tuley and Kornegay do their best to get out of the LVH and home to their families in the foothills bordering the Las Vegas Valley, professional handicapper Steve Fezzik is jumping in his car and leaving his behind.

After spending his day at home making real time bets using apps on his tablet from both the Cantor and William Hill casinos (available only in Nevada, obviously) and beginning to handicap the games that will ultimately form the core of his entry in the upcoming week's SuperContest, Fezzik visits a few casinos that put up irregular and unique bets (called prop – or proposition – bets) for the Sunday night games. Prop bets, such as which team will score first, or kick the first field goal or throw the first interception, resemble bets two fans in a Des Moines basement might create in an attempt to muster energy for one last game after a long day of drinking beer. For a pro like Fezzik, however, prop bets can end up providing more value than a regular point spread bet that has been smoothed and rounded like a river stone washed by millions of bets around the globe.

Fezzik's dash into Las Vegas doesn't mark the end of his day. With a 20-mile drive to the major casinos and the release of spreads for the coming week's games on Sunday evening, it is more like a lunch break. After returning home, there is still live gambling on the Sunday night game, updating power rankings, some family time, another mad scramble to visit casinos where he places a first wave of bets on next week's games as soon as the lines are published and then, finally, some dedicated time watching game replays until he passes out from exhaustion.

>>>>

Until 2001, Steve Fezzik was an insurance executive in Los Angeles, commuting regularly to Las Vegas to gamble. At that point he decided to put his math skills to use as a full time gambler, packed up and came to Las Vegas. In 2008 and 2009, Fezzik became the only back-to-back winner of the LVH Super Contest, an event that changed his life, transforming him from just another professional gambler into a public figure, the guy everyone who participates in the SuperContest hopes to become.

These are undisputed facts, easily validated any number of ways.

However, when it comes to Steve Fezzik, these may be the last indisputable facts.

The SuperContest winner takes home more than a check. He – or potentially she – garners a reputation that can lead to becoming a major player in the sports betting community. Fezzik's two SuperContest wins propelled him to become one of the most recognizable names in sports gambling, a status that makes his name valuable.

Thanks to the internet, anyone making enough income gambling to support themselves can supplement their income through a web site, selling their insights and opinions to others hoping to profit from their experience. Someone like Fezzik, as the only back-to-back winner of the most prestigious football handicapping contest in the world, can find himself in high demand. Such high demand that, apparently, one person isn't enough to meet it.

There is an entire segment of the Las Vegas entertainment industry built around impersonators –– from Cher to Willie Nelson to Tina Turner. However, not everyone wants to be Elvis or some other singer. Some impersonators want to be handicappers, and some of those want to be Steve Fezzik.

There is a stevefezzik.com, not associated with the real Steve Fezzik. There are multiple Twitter accounts claiming to be him that are not associated with the real Steve Fezzik, such as @fezzikfootball, and ironically, @realstevefezzik.

To contact the real Steve Fezzik, I have to submit a blind comment to lvasports.com, the web site where he does offer betting tips. (This includes a large notice on its homepage warning of other sites impersonating him).

His partner replies to me in a matter of minutes and includes Steve's actual email address, along with a reminder that there are imposters pretending to be him.

When I finally reach him via phone, "Steve Fezzik's" voice is awash in the background noise of someone using his car's built-in Bluetooth system. He is open to answering my questions and is free with his time and his opinions – opinions ranging from how I should frame the Super Contest in writing about it, to offering ideas on bets for the coming weekend, to why he has been successful. But any of my requests to meet and talk in person is politely ignored and the subject is rapidly changed.

While talking with him I mentally try to match the voice on the phone with photos of Steve Fezzik on the internet. The most common picture shows a tall, fit man in a polo shirt with a shock of black hair standing with Jay Kornegay and holding an oversized novelty check for $198,600 after his 2009 Super Contest win. The "real" Steve Fezzik's

Twitter account (@fezziksports) includes a picture of the same man, this time pointing at you, wearing an expression common to high powered executives and politicians--a look that says he knows more than you do, so stop wasting his time.

Per his request, our next communication is via email; a list of questions is replied to in a matter of hours, followed closely by a second email with another reminder that there are imposters pretending to be Steve Fezzik.

Apparently if there is a downside of winning nearly $400,000 by successfully selecting NFL game winners 60% of the time across two seasons, it is a lifetime spent reminding others that you are the real you.

Almost lost amidst the identity theft afflicting every aspect of Fezzik's professional life is the simple fact that all this resulted from winning the SuperContest. Perhaps no one has gained and lost more from the SuperContest than Fezzik, yet he has no regrets or concerns about the changing nature of the contest or his continuing participation in it.

Asked about the changes he has seen since first participating, he replies, "It was a local's contest, now everyone is playing it with proxies everywhere."

And the impact of those changes? Positive or Negative? "Super Positive, just like the World Series of Poker main event."

With increased interest in the contest, the geographic footprint of participants has grown. In 2012, a record 745 participants entered, nearly a 50% increase over the previous record. The total payout topped $1 million for the first time.

These numbers aren't feasible with participation limited only to Las

Vegas area residents. Reading about it on Twitter or mainstream media websites fuels interest across the country and the proxy industry popped up to meet the demand.

Vegas Matty is one of those both discussing the SuperContest in social media and benefiting from the boom. He tweets about the SuperContest from his @Vegas_Matty account and since 2005 has been one of the SuperContest's longest-standing and most respected proxies. While he began with only a handful of customers, he and his partner at footballcontestproxy.com now count over 100 clients.

With the use of a local proxy like Vegas Matty to make their weekly submissions, an out-of-state gambler need only come to Las Vegas to pay the entry fee and register prior to the season starting. Then each Wednesday the proxy forwards the official betting card to his customers. The contestant replies with his or her selection by Friday and the proxy submits the card on Saturday morning.

For providing these services – the grunt work of traveling to LVH, filling in the card correctly and submitting the entry every week - Vegas Matty and his partner charge a flat fee and then a small percentage if the customer ends up winning money (he has had a customer in the top ten each of the last three years). While Vegas Matty won't confirm his fees, beyondthebets.com estimates the cost of hiring a proxy service at between $200 and $500 for the season.

᠉᠉᠉

On that same cool, crisp Sunday evening, 625 miles to the east of Las Vegas in Centennial, Colorado, John Turner has put his kids to bed and sits on his couch watching the Sunday night football game. Then the familiar red 'a' on the taskbar of his laptop flashes, indicating an incoming message in AOL Instant Messenger. Co-worker, friend and fellow sports fan, Rodney Peffer, is lamenting a painful loss in the NFL that day from his own home maybe fifteen miles to the east.

Turner and Peffer, like millions of Americans are enjoying their last few hours of a weekend spent shuttling kids between soccer games and softball games and checking off never-ending 'honey-do' lists at home. In between, they have tried to watch as much football as possible.

Soon, the two join a private chat with a 3rd member – me, signing in from Vegas. Turner and Peffer are two of my closest friends and my gambling cohorts.

Both are nearing middle age and are junior executives at a large student loan company. Each man is married with children and has a mortgage on a home in one of the suburbs that encircle Denver. In the past, they sated their gambling jones by playing inconsequential online games all year, with the winner enjoying a free dinner during our annual pilgrimage to Las Vegas where for two days we immersed ourselves in betting on football.

With me as an enabler, my two friends embody the new money coming into the SuperContest. They first became aware of it thanks to Millman and Simmons and, with an increasing interest in all things gambling, the idea of someday participating slowly took hold.

Once I had hatched this plan and told them my idea on the 4th hole of a golf course, they came to the realization that this was their opportunity to join the SuperContest and test their amateur gambling knowledge against real pros. A team of three requires only a $500 investment per person, affordable even with that mortgage and looming college tuition.

Sunday nights have become their one last chance to lick their wounds from near misses earlier in the day and start scouting games for the following weekend's SuperContest entry. John and Rodney act as my control group. Where I spend my week pretending to be a wiseguy, they don't; they go about their daily lives. There are no detailed power rankings to update, complicated spreadsheets to manage or databases of data to pore through. The only tools they use are the games they have watched, the teams' historical performance, the opening spreads reported at a variety of online information sites, and AIM to discuss what they find.

Once the work week begins the next morning, they both know that their opportunity actually to think about which games they like will disappear faster than the lunch they inhale at their desk between meetings. With no pressing deadlines and this weeks' games fresh in their minds, they look for teams to back next week before the final whistle blows for this week.

When the plan was first hatched, despite fantastical ideas of how we would divide a $450,000 first place pay day, neither Turner or Peffer will admit to truly believing we could win against the best handicappers and hundreds of others just like us. Sure, there is the dream scenario where everything goes right but they both knew more than likely that wouldn't occur.

The entry wasn't about making money, it was, as Turner says, "to see how well an above-average NFL fan in terms of following the sport can do actually betting the games against the pros and [determining whether] following the sport translates to betting success." A $500 investment isn't much for the opportunity to rate yourself against the best in the world. How many of us would pay $500 to play a round of golf with Tiger Woods? Or shoot hoops with Michael Jordan?

Plus, there is the T-shirt.

Realistically, they will both admit that placing in the top half of all contestants and maybe just one perfect 5-0 week would constitute a successful first attempt. The first couple months have seen more near-misses than victories but they take solace that they aren't the entrant that compiled a record of 0-9-1 after two weeks.

Separating process from outcome, however, and they admit the contest has already impacted them both. At the halfway point of the season, the contest has already changed how they look at games. As Turner notes, he no longer cheers solely for his favorite team. Now, he is watching any and all teams, regardless of his feelings about them. Rather than hoping for or against a win, he now cares only about performance against the point spread.

Peffer adds, "Just like in poker, you aren't playing your cards, you are playing the other people." In this case, the other people are the casino and the point spread.

"The largest change is going away from what may look obvious at first sight and avoiding the popular teams that are out there to bet on." Turner continues, "It is easy to bet on the Green Bays, Houstons, Patriots, because they typically score a lot of points and are typically near the top of the NFL but you aren't betting on the best teams, you are betting the spread."

Jay Kornegay has also seen a change in the contest with the arrival of more players like the three of us. The most common picks each week in the contest are no longer a proxy for the best bets among wise guys but now resemble a list of most popular and successful NFL teams., ""The consensus picks are totally different than what they were last year [because of the influx of amateurs].... the consensus is the 49ers, Steelers, Eagles, Patriots and Falcons."

We end up chatting throughout the second half of Sunday night football and bounce different points of view off each other. Points are debated, grudges from past wrongs are re-hashed (the Panthers shall never again be trusted after several schizophrenic performances) and by the time we sign off, we each have a pretty good idea which teams we will personally recommend for inclusion on this week's card.

Over the course of the next couple of days, weighing criteria such as the impact of last week's game, rivalry games, and bye weeks, they will each pick their five teams, while I leverage the nascent system I continue to refine. After the official LVH card is released on Wednesday, we will reconvene, review each individual pick and reach a consensus on our five choices for the week. I am then responsible for making over to the LVH to submit our picks before the 11:00 a.m. Saturday deadline – typically on Thursday or Friday afternoon.

Acknowledging the changing nature of the contestants, LVH has made the rules more accommodating to out-of-towners. In the early years, the deadline for submission was Friday night and the cards were never published online, just printed in hard copy and only available at the sports book itself. Now LVH posts the official point spreads online Wednesday nights so that entrants can review them without waiting to see the printed card. They can also make their picks as late as Saturday morning, allowing someone coming into town after work on Friday night to make the deadline.

Where the SuperContest goes from here is anyone's guess. Barring government intervention it is hard to envision the growth ending. It doesn't appear in danger of being beaten by competitors. It has faced a slew of challengers that have tried to supplant it as the premier handicapping contest in Las Vegas – whether through higher stakes to draw only the sharpest of the sharp money or lower stakes to draw anyone willing to shell out less than the cost of an official NFL jersey. None have posed a serious challenge to it, so the question becomes where does the growth end, and does that growth fundamentally change the SuperContest?

Dave Tuley foresees a ceiling around 1,000 participants but he read-ily admits he never expected to see nearly 50% growth between 2011 and 2012. Even if growth slows in the very near future the number of total participants could pass 1,000.

Steve Fezzik welcomes the growth; more participants mean a higher payout. He's loyal and can't envision anything that would end his participation. "I like the management of LVH too much," he says.

Sure, there are increased odds of an amateur riding a hot streak to an unlikely win – a Chris Moneymaker moment, the amateur whose victory in the 2003 World Series of Poker catapulted the event into the national consciousness – but as Dave Tuley notes, historically it has taken at least a 60% win rate to crack the top twenty of the SuperContest and finish in the money, and last years' winner was successful on 72% of his picks. Someone may capture lightning in a bottle occasionally but the odds of an Average Joe winning 60% of his picks in any given year are slim. With only a $1,500 entry, (less than a wise guy normally lays on a single game) and a demonstrable advantage over the majority of bettors, the wise guys know there are few bets with better odds.

Turner and Peffer, two of those amateurs increasing the pot for win-ners this year, are still undecided on whether they want to return in 2013. The deciding factor will likely be our competitiveness as the season reaches its conclusion. Learning by the week, finding a rhythm and achieving more consistent success that pushes us toward the upper-half of the standings may be enough to convince them to make another run next year.

At least that is what they say now. Come July 2013, stranded in the middle of a long, hot summer, facing a football season without the SuperContest to scratch that competitive itch, spending $500 may start to look like a bargain, no matter our performance through the end of 2012. As Peffer noted, "It is cheaper than buying a lotto ticket every week."

Even if we do abstain next year, there are others out there ready to take our place, reading the tweets with updated standings every Sunday night or listening to podcasts while at the gym on Tuesday evening and thinking, "I could do as well as those guys."

Amidst the concerns of running a sports book in a challenging economy, Jay Kornegay isn't focused on growing the contest. There are no major strategic initiatives targeted at the contest. A SuperContest Weekend that was inaugurated at the onset of this season will likely return next year but, beyond that, the contest will continue to be allowed to run and grow organically through word of mouth on social media outlets.

And why should he make changes? When riding a hot streak, sometimes the best thing you can do is to just let it ride.

Week #8

WESTERN KENTUCKY (-7) AT FLORIDA INTERNATIONAL

Yes, the boys are back. A week after they finally couldn't cover in a painful overtime loss to Louisiana-Monroe, the Toppers go on the road to an underperforming FIU team. I think WKU is mad this week and takes it out on Golden Panthers. FIU, a preseason pick to win the Sun Belt have been a big disappointment – losing their last 6 games. They had a chance to break through last week at Troy but fell one point short. If Willie Taggart is the coach that many people believe, he won't let his team wallow in last week's lost opportunity, he will get them up and running this week.

I don't like giving up a touchdown on the road but I am a believer and will ride with Big Red until one of the SEC teams hires Taggart away after the season. Really, this is here mostly because of a lack of other compelling games – either lines that are too high or teams that are too inconsistent – so in the face of uncertainty I turn to a known quantity.

An old belief says that having too much of a good thing can be bad. And this is all you need to know about how I did betting this weekend.

- Spending a weekend with friends – good thing.

- Golfing on an absolutely perfect Las Vegas Friday afternoon – good thing.

- Quality dinner and drinks at Lavo – good thing.

- Walking away from blackjack tables with more chips than I sat down with – good thing.

- Fourteen hours in a sports book watching college football – good thing.

- Betting on games for fourteen hours just to have some action on the in-progress games – too much of a good thing.

My fall in Vegas to date has been defined by discipline and moderation. Writing every day. Working out a few times per week. Eating at home most of the time. No income and months of bets looming have caused me also to be disciplined in my betting. I have barely sat at a blackjack table. I have not been throwing bet after bet just for entertainment sake. I have found my shortlist of spreads that I like each week and put my money there.

I have also used this approach in deciding on when to spend time in a sports book. I can't handle fourteen hours each week in a sports book, so I have picked my visits to coincide with the games where I have the most at stake. Maybe I drop down to the MGM for the 12:30 slate of games. Maybe a field trip to Aria or Mandalay for the prime-time games. But never do I take a seat at 8:00 a.m., and not depart until after 8:00 p.m. My lungs and wallet could never survive that much exposure to smoke and gambling opportunities.

But that was when I was alone. When visitors arrive for their annual Vegas boys' weekend, priorities change. Discipline is thrown out with last week's groceries. Weeks of avoiding blackjack tables lasts less than twelve hours. Lavish dinners are enjoyed. Most importantly, dumb bets are made in the name of fun.

With Turner, Peffer and another friend in town for the weekend, we commandeered a table in the Mandalay Bay sports book before Lee Corso had donned his headgear and didn't relinquish it until we had to keep Turner from jumping out the 19th floor window of his hotel room after Notre Dame beat Oklahoma. Despite laying my best bets earlier in the week and chasing games on Thursday and Friday I continued to lay more bets throughout the day, just for the fun of it. This is what you do on vacation in Vegas. Where the rest of the season has been business; this weekend was for fun.

Which is a good thing because if this was a business, it lost more money than the entire Silicon Valley combined in 2001.

There is no reason for me to re-cap all of my bad bets here – just know I lost because of the lack of weather in Colorado (see: Air Force vs Nevada total points), lack of offense at Iowa, lack of defense by Houston and lack of talent by Mississippi State.

But make no mistake, I lost and lost frequently. If there was any bet that symbolized my day it was North Carolina State vs North Carolina.

I loved getting the Wolfpack as more than a touchdown underdog (+7.5). I just couldn't see the Tar Heels blowing them out and was validated when the line moved down to +7 after I laid the bet. Naturally the Tar Heels came out and dominated early, jumping to a 25-7 lead and my smugness at getting a good line ended rather quickly.

NC State rallied and took 35-25 lead into the 4th quarter. When UNC kicked a field goal to tie the game with less than two minutes to play, I figured I was set. Neither team was scoring multiple times, I could go ahead and cash. And then the inexplicable happened.

NC State punted back to UNC inside of the final 30 seconds and Giovanni Bernard returned it for a touchdown with 13 seconds to play. But, hey that's ok. My bet is on NC State at +7.5. A touchdown can't beat me, this is why I am so brilliant for getting the line at more than 7.

<Cue me high fiving Turner and Shadow, and digging another beer out of our bucket, congratulating myself for buying at the right line.>

<Sips beer, glances up to screen to await final whistle to cash ticket>

"UNC winning 43-35...wait...does that say UNC is leading by 8? How is that....WHAT THE HELL ... HOW AM I GOING TO LOSE?!?!"

I still don't know what happened but UNC scored a 2-point conversion. Whether bad snap or designed play, I don't know. Since everyone outside the Clark County sees it as a meaningless detail, no write-ups provide an explanation.

But at least NC State losing puts FSU back in line to play the ACC title game.

Yes, I am grasping for positives after a long string of losses.

In the end, though, all of those losses served a valuable purpose. They reinforced the discipline required to win in the long term in the sports book. You can't survive a 13-week college football season or 20-week NFL season throwing cash at every single game and hope it sticks. You need to find the ones you feel most confident in and hit them hard. Even when the teams I publicly picked won I failed to make much money. Yes, Western Kentucky won but one step forward doesn't accomplish much when you are sent sailing backwards by a tidal wave.

At this point, WKU should probably put me on payroll as their personal publicist. Each week I bet them and write about them and then each week I win. I should have known that even as almost every game worked against me this weekend, the Hilltoppers would come through. If I were time traveling to the island from Lost, 'Hilltoppers covering the spread' would be my constant.

I have already bought Hilltopper t-shirts for Turner, Peffer and I, so I am not sure what else I can do to show my appreciation. I guess I could donate a building or endow a chair or something.

After publicly saying I loved Kent State at Rutgers, I never bet on the Flashes (I wanted to get it above 14 points), so despite calling it I didn't bet it, outside of a three team tease. Brilliant work by me. For those that missed it, yes Kent State covered rather easily. In fact, they won going away so my original pick would have easily won and even a Moneyline at somewhere around +425 would have cashed. Yet, I only picked them in a bet tied to both WKU and Marshall also doing well.

We all know WKU is practically free money, so all I needed was Marshall to hang with an up and down UCF team at home.

Which they did, for about a quarter. Before getting blown off their own field 54-17.

It stinks to be completely wrong about a game or team and lose money on them. It is much worse to be right about a team and still lose money on them. But at least my instincts were right – I saw value on Kent State and was ultimately proven right.

Yes, I am grasping for positives after...ahh, forget it. I had fun, even if I did lose money.

SAN DIEGO (-2.5) AT CLEVELAND

After the Chargers' epic Monday Night Meltdown a couple weeks ago, I don't think there is much of a feeling for the Chargers in Vegas. Are they the traditionally solid team we have seen over the last decade? Is the Norv/Rivers era over? No one is quite sure. Even in the best of times, when they were an annual Super Bowl contender they would hit bad spots and play like the 30th best team in the league, so calling the end of an era is really tough mid-season.

I think this line is an overreaction to that Rivers meltdown against the Broncos. Teams coming off a bye (by my math) are 7-3 this season against the spread. The Chargers have had to stew on that loss and the subsequent jokes for two weeks. They are rested and ready to make a statement. We have all watched enough episodes of the Rivers & Norv Show to recognize this is a game where they traditionally dominate a weaker opponent so that we again debate whether they are the class of the AFC West.

If it isn't; if the Chargers again look lost, well then we also learned something else. That the Rivers & Norv Show only has nine episodes left.

MIAMI (+2) AT NY JETS

These two teams are the exact opposite in a lot of ways. The Jets seems to value attention over performance – preferring to make headlines rather than touchdowns. The Dolphins, despite being on Hard

Knocks, have gone practically unnoticed all season. Sneaky (against the spread) wins against the Cardinals and Bengals and then a near (ATS) miss against the Rams at home, the Dolphins are a little better than the sum of their parts. The offense, made up of a rookie quarterback, cast-off running back and no-name wide receivers is offset by the 8th ranked defense in the league. A defense on which you can name no members. Don't even pretend.

The Dolphins, coming off a bye (see a pattern here?) get to take on a Jets team deflated by the near miss at New England last week. Beating up on a bad Pats secondary doesn't solve the Jets problems – no running game and inconsistent quarterback play. It just gives the Jets another week in the headlines.

Of further note is that the Jets are in the week prior to their bye. Add a secondary trend if you want but the record of teams in the week prior to their bye is horrid this year (1-13). Basically you get two trends for the price of one on this game! It's like buying a fitted tweed sportcoat and getting a free AWOL Nation CD!

I hope this line moves over +3 but even if it doesn't I like the Dolphins to win outright.

There are four words that are the most painful thing you can say to a sports bettor.

No, not "You're broke, stop betting," because don't you worry about that. I still have that baseball card collection at my parents' house and that is worth thousands, THOUSANDS, so don't worry about me.

No, I was thinking of 'regression to the mean.'

For those who have a decade or two separating you from that college statistics course you used to sleep through, this basically means that a short term trend will regress back to its long term average over time. You may flip a coin five times and end up with five straight heads, but that doesn't mean the odds are different all of a sudden. Keep flipping long enough and it will slowly migrate back to 50/50.

And so it is with betting trends.

Underdogs covering at an abnormally high rate early in the season? Sooner or later, that is coming back down.

Teams coming off a bye with a great record against the spread? Good luck, calling the peak of that market.

And so that is the dilemma we faced this weekend. The first half of the season showed some definite trends. But do they continue or revert back to their historical trend pattern? And if so, when?

A few weeks ago I watched games with Dave Tuley, who is a big NFL underdog bettor. He rode that trend to 4th place in the LVH SuperContest before last week. Then went 1-4. Does this mean that the favorites are more likely to cover going forward? No. it just means we should expect it to go back to its historic relationship.

So, what does this mean for a gambler? Try to time the market on trends or stick with the fundamentals, which are ironically, a lot less 'fun.'

Up until this point, we have stuck with the fundamentals. Looking for value, where the difference between two teams is greater than the point spread. Its success could best be described as 'mehh.'

So, this week I rode a couple trends and hoped we didn't jump on that wave just as it petered out at the shoreline. But, unsure on calling the peak of the wave and coming off a miserable Saturday betting, I stayed conservative. In short, I chickened out this weekend.

There were games I liked, that my 'system' said had value, yet I didn't bet, or didn't bet enough or tied it to other outcomes, stupidly chasing a bigger payday. There were also games where I was just plain wrong, where I relied on gut or instinct or even my system and was wrong. I can't do much about those. But to have left money on the table when everything about a game said to bet it big is the frustrating part.

Coming off a tough day on Saturday at Mandalay, we decided to go all George Costanza and do the reverse on Sunday – by traveling to the opposite end of the Strip to watch games at the LVH.

In the summer, after a rain-soaked afternoon on a golf course, as Turner, Peffer and I sat around a restaurant table we discussed what might happen as part of this little experiment of mine. Of the many dreams that were discussed – like what to do with the $450,000 after we win the SuperContest – one random request was made by Rodney. In between bites of fish taco, Rodney said, "My goal for you, is that by the time we visit in October, you walk in somewhere and are greeted with 'Hello, Mr. McIntire'."

We all harbored a dream of being an insider in Vegas, being catered to by personalized service thanks to our importance. But with only a handful of trips per year and an unwillingness to bet the thousands required to be a big fish, we had grown accustomed to being the invisible majority when it comes to the real service at casinos on the Strip. With one of us 'going local' maybe we would finally be welcomed into the club. At least that was the hope.

In addition to writing this book, I also wrote freelance articles while in Vegas. In part this was to increase my profile—to improve the odds of seeing this diatribe actually published. It was also a tangible excuse to meet some of the industry insiders, the people with the history and experience in this world that I would never gain in six months.

The first half of this chapter was the first such effort. Through the research for that article I met and interviewed Jay Kornegay who runs the LVH sportsbook. Jay, who grew up in Colorado before coming to Las Vegas, has become one of the most sought after people in the sports betting universe. The LVH is constantly on the cutting edge of sports betting and his point of view is requested regularly by radio shows, writers and podcasters across the country. That doesn't stop him from being incredibly nice to know-nothing people like me and generous with his time. In the wake of that interview (but prior to publication), I reached back out to Jay and asked if it would be possible to get VIP passes for the weekend when John and Rodney visited town. Jay agreed easily. While this seems rather shady – I write article about your contest, you give me free food and drink - in my defense, Dave Tuley, who I had also interviewed, actually suggested reaching out to Jay about passes. Also, I am a businessman, not a journalist, so my ethics on such things are much less rigid.

❧❧❧

Sunday the sun rose over Las Vegas on another cool, pleasant late fall morning. Men began flowing through the door of Football Central at 9:00 a.m., walking past a display of merchandise: signed pictures, balls and other memorabilia. In a steady stream of jerseys and team-centric T-shirts, they flow from the bright, loud, smoky casino floor into the dark of the theater.

They mostly travel in groups and discuss with their cohorts what games look most appealing on these menus of hoped-for riches. There are the overly loud packs of younger men -- probably still drunk from their big Saturday night in Vegas – many sipping beer from the cheap plastic cups, trying to drown out the impending trip home. Other groups sip coffee from Styrofoam cups and talk in low tones, wearing the weary expressions of locals resigned to being constantly surrounded by vacationers.

On the wall at the front of the theater, pre-game shows cut through the darkness, desks of large men in suits, yelling over each other and laughing uproariously at mildly humorous comments. With the games an hour away from kick-off, that is just background noise. The men in the jerseys and team shirts that occupy the padded seats stretching from wall to wall pay little attention to the screens. Head down, they study parlay cards and betting sheets and rarely look up. They hope such focus enables them to divine the best bet available.

At the entrance to Football Central, in his blue and orange John Lynch jersey, Jay greets arrivals. He will spend his morning ensuring everything is operating smoothly and that the VIPs are being well taken care of. In between catching pieces of the games he will sneak back to the glass-walled computer room to check on how the lines are sitting and where the money is flowing.

As we walked up, two of us in Bronco shirts ourselves, Jay put his hand out and greeted me with a "Hey, David." I shook it, introduced my friends, and thanked him while he asked one of his employees to give us our bands. For once we were the insiders. As we headed up the stairs to the balcony past the 'authorized personnel only' sign, we had finally accomplished something in Vegas. As far as John and Rodney were concerned, this trip was a success whether a word of this or anything else I write ever sees the light of day.

With comped food and drink all day and a mostly deserted balcony at our disposal, we were home for the day. We ultimately stayed from an hour before kick off until nearly the end of the afternoon games, with the only departures from our empty row being trips to the restroom, betting window or back for more food and drinks. It was a perfect way to spend an NFL Sunday with friends. Except in one way: again, I wasn't winning a lot.

I ended up only betting on the Dolphins at New York as part of a three-team tease with Denver and Atlanta. All three of the teams were coming off a bye and absolutely dominated their opponents, winning by a combined 94-40. Even after my glowing write-up of Miami before the weekend, I never bet them alone, afraid that the Jets may actually show up for a game well prepared. Silly me.

Rather than betting these teams alone, I combined them into a single tease where I moved the lines down. Sure, it paid better than a single bet would, but had I trusted myself and also bet one or more of these games alone I could have doubled my winnings from a single accurate prediction.

Instead I placed individual bets on two other teams coming off byes – San Diego (-3) at Cleveland and Kansas City (-2) at Oakland.

Teams coming off a bye have been inordinately successful so far this season – 7-3 coming into this weekend. Of course none of those teams were the worst team in the league (Kansas City) or a team that is using years of good performance as a camouflage for the fact that they have a bad defense, no offensive weapons, and an incompetent coach (San Diego).

These bets both lost after two remarkable no-shows. Kansas City lost at home to an equally abysmal Raiders team 26-16 and the Chargers lost 7-6 at Cleveland in the remnants of a hurricane. Where other teams took their bye week to rejuvenate tired bodies, get over injuries and re-focus for the remainder of the season, I am pretty sure that the Chiefs and Chargers just used that extra time to catch up on episodes of Honey Boo Boo that they missed preparing for previous games.

It was a good thing the beer was free at LVH. With all these losses I couldn't have afforded all of the beer I needed to drown my sorrows.

Addendum (January 4, 2013)

Is there anything better than unexpected good news?

This morning, I woke up planning to spend my morning at an auto shop getting a minor but annoying issue with my car fixed. It seemed to my unsophisticated eye to be a simple fix, but I am jaded to expect the worst any time I walk in to a mechanic, where seemingly no matter the issue, I drive out hours (if not days) later hundreds of dollars poorer.

So, I didn't start the day in the best of mindsets, until I got an email from Rodney, one of my partners in our LVH SuperContest entry, Team THH. In addition to the season long contest, in which our entry has been mired somewhere below the mean all season, this year SuperContest instituted a mini-contest for early joiners. The entry (or entries) with the best aggregate records across the final three weeks of the season would win $10,000. With no shot at the big money, we focused on this as a chance to get our money back.

Week #15: We started off well with a 4-1 week, our 2nd or 3rd 4-1 week of the season, our only loss being the New York Giants getting thumped by Atlanta. But at 4-1, along with about 100 other entries we were at least still in the discussion

Week #16: We assumed our dream ended with a 3-2 week after the Bucs decided to finish the season two weeks early and got blown out at home by the Rams. The Giants poured salt on our wound by losing again – this time getting blown out in Baltimore. With three losses and several teams with one or two losses we abandoned hope of finishing in the money in the Mini-contest.

With no chance at money we had three goals with week #17 remaining (1) just one 5-0 week, (2) get our record above .500 across the contest and (3) finish in the top 50% of the contest.

Week #17 – Things started well for us. Indianapolis easily covers their +6.5 spread, winning the game outright. Buffalo blows out the Jets, thanks to yet another fine show of incompetence by Mark Sanchez and the Titans dominate the Jaguars. With the morning gone, we are 3-0. In the afternoon session, after Houston's loss, the Patriots come out and dominate the Dolphins, ensuring a bye week and #2 seed in the playoffs. 4-0 with only the Redskins as 3-point favorites at home against the Cowboys remaining.

The Redskins hold a 3 point lead over the Cowboys with three and a half minutes remaining and it sure appears that at best we will get a push and a 4-0-1 week. But then Tony Romo does Tony Romo things to start the drive where he has a chance to win the game and propel the Cowboys to the playoffs –lofting a pass to the flat that is intercepted by the Redskins. Deep in the Cowboys' end, the Redskins can either run out the clock, kick a gimme field goal if unable to gain a first down or score a touchdown. Ultimately, they score the touchdown, giving them a ten-point win and giving Team THH a 5-0 week. Miracle one is completed.

The perfect score has also gotten us above .500 on the season: 42-41-2. Miracle #2.

After some virtual rejoicing, we all move on with our lives – I moved on to the bowl games that pepper the next two days. Rodney and John turned to family, football and then work.

It was just this morning, as part of an on-going email exchange, I asked Rodney if he had ever gone back to check how we'd ended up in the final standings – could we really finish in the upper half of the 745 entrants?

It was a link in his response that added a couple watts to the blinding Vegas sun outside. A link to the LVH website showing the Final SuperContest and Mini-Contest standings. There atop the Mini-contest standings, the top name among the 18 teams that tied with the same score and would therefore share the Mini-contest $10,000 prize was the name Team THH.

Not only had we finished with a 5-0 record, got above .500 for the season and ended in the top half of all entrants (349 of 745 – Miracle #3), we somehow clawed back into a tie for the Mini-contest prize.

Miracle #4 – more than enough miracles for us to be sanctified.

We didn't win the $450,000 SuperContest first prize but we never expected to. However, at most, 38 of the 745 entrants got any money back from the LVH SuperContest this season, and we were one. Our $525 prize ($10,000 split 18 ways), barely covers one-third of our entry fee, but this is probably the most satisfying win of the season for me. We joined the contest to play with the big boys and succeeded in every way imaginable.

I am already looking forward to the planning for next season that will occur at our celebratory dinner this weekend.

Oh, and at the auto shop, five minutes of work fixed my problem at no cost.

The Losing Streak

In America these days, there is no better way to get ahead than to loudly and proudly make the most ridiculous argument possible. There are cable channels where the entire business model has shifted from reporting news to creating arguments and debates out of thin air. Solid thinking and reasonable stances can never stand out in a crowded marketplace of ideas. It is the loudest and most outrageous that now gains the most attention. Intelligence has been replaced by volume.

On TV this has led to someone like Skip Bayless having made a lucrative career from constantly yelling an unpopular, usually ridiculously stupid opinion and vociferously defending it. In fact, for the most part, Skip doesn't appear to know the word 'opinion.' In his world everything he utters is fact. He appears multiple times per day on the largest sports channel in the world and his income is reportedly around $500,000 per year. All for being loud, ignorant and proud.

On the internet, often it isn't the smartest or most interesting work that gains the most attention. Instead it is the most inane article, written almost openly to invite derision and mockery, that gains the most pageviews. And, no this isn't just an elaborate excuse to explain the non-existent audience of my web site.

There are 'sports' websites, who spend as much space on women in bikinis as they do on actually reporting on sports, because they know there is a segment that will click on any article that provides the cheap thrill of seeing a beautiful woman wearing little.

Bryan Stow gets beaten into a coma at a Giants/Dodgers game and someone writes an article blaming Stow for wearing a baseball jersey to the game. Colin Kaepernick takes over a starting job and adds a new dimension to the Forty-Niners' offense yet a columnist says the tattoos on his arms are a disgrace. These aren't reasonable or even necessary articles. They are just 'different' takes on current news, meant more to bring attention to the writer than to actually advance the sports conversation. In both of those real-life examples, the writer gained more attention than they ever would have had they written intelligent, thought-provoking articles. Sure they were widely ridiculed, but they still got those pageviews. There are a hundred other sites providing a good perspective, there aren't 100 others advancing the most ridiculous thought in the country. Guess which one gets the clicks?

Outside of women in bikinis there is no better guarantee of attention than claiming you can help someone win money betting on sports. You don't need to study Maslow's Hierarchy of Needs to recognize that sex and money are the two lowest common denominators to successfully get attention. Combine them both and you end up with the 'Handicapping Hotties' which really exists and is exactly what you think it is. It isn't a coincidence that professional gamblers that sell their picks are called 'touts. ' They need to spend as much or more time touting their success as they do actually handicapping.

But there is one easy way to reduce the chances of falling for someone's false stories of their own gambling genius - ask them what percentage of bets they win. The higher their answer, the better the chance they have no idea what they are doing and/or don't even bet.

No one ever wins every bet they lay. As I have told my friends repeatedly, they don't build these palaces out here handing out money. If someone is constantly bragging about their outlandish handicapping successes, they are either (1) completely full of it or (2) selectively only talking about their hot streaks. Either way, you can be pretty sure they are nowhere near as successful as they pretend to be.

Here is a quick reality check. The very best gamblers in the world, the few men who can actually make a living solely by gambling win fewer than 60% of their bets. An NFL season at 60% winning would be historically successful. Yet, every day you meet or read online about people that claim to win 75% or 80% of their bets. They may do this in some small sample size - hell, even I have weeks where I win all my bets - but no one does this in any sustained way. Nobody.

To make a long term profit a gambler needs to win 52.4% of their bets (assuming bets are all the same amount). But no one always wins 52.4% or more of their bets. Anyone that bets for any period of time will have periods of success and periods of failure. Even for the best in the world, a losing streak is a fact of life. It is the reaction of pro gamblers to the inevitable losing streak that separates them from the rest of us.

When all of us amateurs hit a cold streak, we either walk away completely (especially if our bankroll is now gone) or do a 180 turn on our approach. I am as guilty as anyone here. There have been times where I have actually said to myself 'Well, I think Team A is going to win, so that guarantees that Team B will win.' That is just how it feels. Times when everything looks right, something goes wrong and you lose. The times when you get dealt two Kings at a blackjack table yet fully expect the dealer to get a twenty-one.

It is easy to think that if you are consistently wrong, you are at fault and need to change everything you do. However, this is really more a symptom of the core problem – laying bets based on nothing more than a gut feeling. When you don't have an underlying basis for your picks beyond what you think will happen, a cold streak just means your gut is wrong. It is much easier to lose all confidence in picks when there isn't some quantitative basis for your picks.

It was no coincidence that, while I have faced cold streaks throughout this season, the worse cold streaks have all been in college football. In the NFL, I rely on a quantitative system but in college, my basis is really driven by personal opinion and performance to date. I don't have spreadsheets that measure the validity of point spreads, I have my opinion and a little bit of data on how the teams have performed so far this season. It shouldn't be a surprise that there are inflection weeks in which my opinion is universally wrong. The books are learning as quickly as I am; where I saw value they saw losses. They aren't going to continue making the same mistake the entire season. It was my inability to adapt that led to a few losses and then to a cold streak.

Really the most unfortunate thing about my losing streak was that it occurred at the same time I had friends visiting so I spent more time in the sports books, and bet more than I typically do. Thus I compounded a lost weekend by chasing action when on other weekends I would have gone home quietly.

Pros see a cold streak as the cost of doing business. Do they enjoy it? Of course not. But neither do they throw away all of the work they have done in the face of losing. With a system evolved over time, based on experience that has shown itself to be successful, there is no returning to the drawing board. On the other hand, making no changes isn't a tenable strategy either. Complacency is the enemy, as I proved. Wiseguys therefore look to take an Adapt and Adjust approach.

By this approach I mean that they maintain the same core system but look for a new piece of the puzzle that might have been missing before. Was there an element not being accounted for in the system? Tweaking and modifying the system, or adding a new element can limit the impact of a losing streak.

As for me? My core system wasn't changed in the face of a losing streak; however, I did make one adjustment. When holding a ticket that looked like a winner but could still lose, I bet the opposite as a hedge at halftime of the game. Sure, it cost me some winnings but it guaranteed a win. Having not had the opportunity to cash a ticket in a while, I was more than happy to cash a winner for a smaller amount.

Week #9

KENT STATE (-20) VS AKRON
As discussed before, Kent State has been great against the spread (7-1 on the season) and come home after a shocking upset at Rutgers last week to play a very weak Akron team. As much as this is a show of confidence in Kent State, it is also a point spread play. Keeping it under 21 is important to minimize the chance of some random late-game, garbage Zips touchdown ruining what should be a comfortable win.

Also, of note: donbest.com ranks Kent State as 27 points better than Akron, so there is that.

ILLINOIS (+27) VS OHIO STATE
In 2004, I voted for John Kerry. I was never a big fan of Kerry but compared to the alternative he was the logical choice for me. Now, this isn't to point out the incredible number of similarities between Kerry and Mitt Romney, but it is to point out that sometimes, picking one side is more about who you go against as opposed to who you support.

If you read the above paragraph as an attempt to distance myself from actually endorsing the Illini…well, no comment. Look, I know the Illini stink. I get it.

However, I am writing this because Ohio State has been dreadful against big spreads this year. In fact, dreadful might be understatement. Let's take a quick trip down memory lane for the Buckeyes this year:

- *Week #2 vs. UCF: 16 point favorite. Won by 15*

- *Week #3 vs. Cal: 17 point favorite. Won by 7*

- *Week #4 vs. UAB: 35 point favorite. Won by 14*

"But...but..." you say "Those were all early season. Now after several more weeks under Urban Meyer, surely they are as rock solid against big spreads as Urban is in putting his family above his job."

Well, let me continue, Mr. Impatient.

Week #7 at Indiana: 19 point favorite. Won by 3

"Yeah, but on the road is..."

AHEM, Week #8 vs Purdue: 17 point favorite. Won by 7.

"Oh"

So, to answer your question, yes they are as solid as Urban Meyer is in putting family first (In that both constantly fail).

ꙩꙩꙩꙩ

It seems fitting to look back at Election week with the words of a President and the founding document of our fine country:

"We hold these truths to be self-evident…"

While, good old Thomas Jefferson was talking about the rights of men to carry on affairs with slave women and drink French wine without the interference of a far-away King (or something), I am instead applying them today to my bets on college football.

For the truths I held to be self-evident yesterday are no longer truths. Much like Mitt Romney's ideologies, the things I believed yesterday – that I knew in the deepest corner of my heart – are no longer. Gone faster than if a pollster told me they wouldn't help me get elected President.

My crowning achievement – profiting from the Western Kentucky Hilltoppers – like Romneycare, is now something to distance myself from. To pretend that things have changed.

I sit here a humbled man. I stuck to the strength of my convictions and in the end I lost.

Let's hope I have at least one of those things in common with Romney.

The lesson I take from another week of blanket losses is that where I saw value before, Vegas has adjusted. Tired of giving away money by underestimating smaller teams though they were consistently beating the spreads, Vegas is now overrating those teams. Putting up big spreads and daring them to win big.

I, unfortunately, rode the wave for one week too long and it deposited me headfirst on the beach. I stuck with the teams even against bigger spreads and they failed me. Vegas has adjusted and now I must do the same, for where one window of value has closed another door of value must have opened.

My weekend of losses started early. With another set of friends in town for the weekend I went to dinner at the Palazzo on Thursday night while Western Kentucky kicked off at home against Middle Tennessee State as 9.5 point favorites.

I have stuck with the Hilltoppers for weeks. Through thick and thin. Yet, after this week, I think it is time we took a break. Playing a decent but inconsistent MTSU team at home they not only failed to cover the spread but lost outright 34-29, which tells me that the Sun Belt might have figured out the Hilltoppers. Combining that with Vegas affording them more respect after their remarkable fifteen game against-the-spread win streak and I think we can officially say there is little value on the Hilltoppers at this point.

Thanks for all you have done, Hilltoppers. I wish you luck in all your future endeavors.

On Saturday, my losses continued as another stalwart couldn't come through when I needed them most. Kent State actually fell behind a bad Akron team 24-14, presumably in an early game let-down after their big road win at Rutgers. A second half rally netted them an 11-point win but not enough to cover the massive 20-point spread and the large amount of respect they now commandeer in Vegas.

Having to say goodbye to both WKU and Kent State in the same week is tough. Like saying goodbye to old friends. This must be how Mitt felt when he abandoned every belief he held as Governor of Massachusetts in a bid to be palatable in a Republican Presidential primary.

My bad afternoon continued. After a short stint enjoying the sun at the pool, I came back to the condo to check in on Illinois and Ohio State.

The surest bet on the board this season has been Ohio State failing to meet the high spreads put on them against weak competition. I jumped on this bet early, afraid it would drop below 24, getting it at 24.5. Instead it promptly went above 27, demonstrating that the guys behind the counter had also noticed OSU's weak performance in big spread games and arbitrarily set the bar too low. Despite power rankings showing OSU being 27 points better than the Illini, the books opened at 24, presumably because they don't trust the Buckeyes to cover either.

When Illinois scored a touchdown on a fumble return with five minutes to play, they closed the lead down to 23 and I thought I might escape with a cheap cover. Instead, after a failed onside kick gave OSU a short field, the Buckeyes' back-ups ran it right through the Illinois defense for a final minute touchdown and a 30-point victory.

That will teach me to bet on a school that fired Ron Zook and somehow got worse.

Still hurting from losses piling up faster than Republicans positioning themselves for a Presidential run in 2016, I went to Lagasse Stadium to meet friends for dinner and the evening games--games that have been marked on every college football fan's calendar since the season kicked off: Alabama at LSU and Oregon at USC.

Lagasse's Stadium in the bottom level of the Palazzo has become the standard bearer for luxury sports book game viewing in Las Vegas. But with that luxury comes a high price tag. The main area of the Stadium consists of rows of couches built on an incline like a theater. Each couch has its own table and an unobstructed view of a giant bank of TVs, with betting boards off to the side.

What separates Lagasse's Stadium from other sports books is the cost. Where every other sports book allows anyone to sit on a first come, first served basis with no expectation on spending, Lagasse's requires minimum food and drink purchases for any of the main areas during prime viewing time.

For a couch in the main theater that cost is $100 per person per game. For the couch areas in the bar or one of the tables it drops to $50 per person per game. For the boxes it is considerably more (for the BCS national title game, a box that seats ten will cost $2,000).

The theater seats are great with perfect sight lines to both TVs and betting boards. But the number of TVs is relatively limited, so if you have money on a Sun Belt game you can forget about watching it. The boxes and couch areas near the bar have a dedicated TV per section in which you get to choose what is broadcast. But if you are looking to track two games, you either need to strike a deal with your neighbor or hope you have a lucky view of a random TV not in your section.

If you are willing to pay for it, the seating is as comfortable as they come: big, soft couches and low tables. If you aren't in a reserved couch section, you are stuck at a crowded, tight bar or at one of the basic dining tables, which is just like sitting at a sports bar for three hours.

Having reservations, thanks to some high-roller friends staying at the hotel (comped, by the way), we avoided the line out the door and piled onto couches on the top level of the two story stadium behind the bar. A group of six, we had two couches and two TVs at our disposal. With food and drink minimums to hit, we went through multiple rounds of beer and several orders of the upscale bar food that lines the menu while watching the games.

Coming off the bad week so far, I bet little on the two marquee games. I put a small bet on the LSU money line at +300. When LSU took a second half lead late into the fourth quarter , I was less than two minutes from being dead right but (once again) fell short. Alabama's last minute touchdown gave them the win 21-17 but didn't cover the game's 8-point spread. My visiting friends had significantly more riding on the Tide winning and covering, so the end result of a close Alabama win was pretty much the worst of both worlds for our little corner of Lagasse Stadium.

Grasping at straws to record any kind of win on the day – which is the absolute worst reason possible to lay a bet – I took a flyer on a second half parlay of USC (+3) and Under of 40 total points.

Trailing by 10 at half, I expected USC to make some adjustments, slow the Oregon offense and make a small comeback. They were at home and had beaten Oregon the previous year. They knew how to play with the Ducks. Or so, I thought.

Again, I was only partially right. USC and Oregon traded scores throughout the second half and a 10 point halftime deficit turned into an 11 point USC loss, so my +3 on USC covered. Unfortunately, that score trading also meant that the ludicrously high second half Over/Under was blown out of the water when the teams combined for 55 points.

It was fitting to lose one last bet by being almost completely right.

Baltimore (-3.5) at Cleveland

Cleveland has become a bad team that is trendy to like. After their home win against the Chargers last week, the common theory is that their defense is better than expected, Brandon Weeden is growing into his starting role, and Trent Richardson is a young Adrian Peterson. Combine that with a questionable Ravens' offense and a defense whose plan for stopping a running game is to wave a red cape in front of the running back and this looks like a prime underdog candidate.

I am not fully buying it. The Browns can compete but it sure helps to play a disheartened Chargers team with no running game in the midst of a hurricane. The Ravens are coming off a bye, so they have had an extra week to start to get healthy as well as scheme around the holes created by the season ending injuries seen recently.

This is also the confluence of two trends this season: teams going into a bye playing poorly and teams coming out of a bye playing great.

I think the Ravens are mad that we have all spent the last two weeks stabbing their playoff prospects in the ribs with a knife, Ray Lewis style. They want to come out and make us forget about their recent poor play in the same way that Lewis has re-crafted legacy from felon to inspirational leader.

THREE TEAM TEASE: MIAMI (+3.5) AT INDIANAPOLIS, ATLANTA (+1.5) VS DALLAS, TAMPA BAY (+7.5)

I liked the Florida teams on the road because they are better teams and the teased line crosses the 3-point line for Miami and 7-point line for Tampa. There is a chance that Andrew Luck finds a way to beat the Dolphins, but they have been good on the road against the spread, so I will ride them for one more week.

For weeks, I kept falling for the Falcons as a big home favorite and for weeks they failed to cover. Apparently I wasn't the only one, because they opened at only -4.5 this week. Part of that are the casinos hedging against the popularity of the Cowboys but I think part of it was the realization that the Falcons just can't dominate teams in the Georgia Dome. They may have the first home disadvantage in league history. So, fool me once, Falcons, but like George W. Bush tried to say, 'I won't be fooled again'. Yes, I will pick you at home, but only a line teased to allow you to even lose by 1 and still cover.

All cold snaps must come to an end. Unless we are entering a new ice age of gambling, sooner or later sanity will return and with it some profits. In the end, the lesson of this week was that logic and statistics will always win in the end.

Nate Silver has been under attack from those that didn't agree with his mathematical models that predicted the precise comfortable Obama win we witnessed. Professional talking heads, paid to use no logic or reason to loudly reach a definitive conclusion refused to acknowledge the math underpinning everything. Like a painful replay of major league baseball in 2001, a line was drawn between the 'believers' and the 'calculators.'

But this isn't about the election or sabermetrics. This is about football. And in a neat bit of correlation, the NFL saw the same return to logic this weekend.

Early in the season, the NFL had been dominated by underdogs. The underdogs had won more than 60% of the time this season. This weekend, though, finally saw the 'regression to the mean' that statisticians worship. Favorites went 11-3 this weekend against the spread. The underdogs have still won around 58% of games this year, but we are marching back to historical equilibrium.

We can yell and scream about why we think the underdogs were winning, but in the end it was going to end sooner or later.

Unlike us, math doesn't have emotions or motivations.

How do you know things have changed? Sign #1 is that blindly betting all of my best bets this week would have won every single bet – and paid handsomely doing it.

My biggest bet of the day featured a team who has been a disappointment recently (Baltimore) and a team that has pleasantly surprised

(Cleveland). It also featured a team coming off a bye (Baltimore) against a team about to go on a bye (Cleveland). In short, everything pointed to Baltimore as a 3.5 favorite as too small.

When Baltimore jumped to a 14-0 lead, the bet looked like it might be cashed by halftime. Cleveland crawled back by dominating the weak Ravens run defense but couldn't score touchdowns and went to half trailing 14-9.

Coming off a bad couple of days with no wins, I decided to hedge a little at half and took Cleveland as a pick-em (but paying +105). This guaranteed a win for me no matter what occurred in the 2nd half. Even if the hedge was only a quarter of the original bet, I wanted a win.

In the end I didn't need it as the Ravens finally got the offense moving again late in the 2nd half after Cleveland briefly took a 1-point lead, 15-14. Baltimore scored a touchdown to take the lead back and then got an interception that resulted in a field goal to clinch the game, 25-15. It wasn't pretty (nothing in the AFC North ever is) but after going 0-fer on Saturday I was happy to win my first bet of the day.

I followed up the Baltimore win with another win on a last minute bet thrown down in the ruins of a lost Saturday night in the sports book. I laid a bet on Seattle (-4.5) at home against Minnesota with the simple logic of: very good home team + road team struggling on offense = a win by more than four. Sometimes things work out as planned, even when Adrian Peterson runs around and over the Seahawks defense like he is working on a cone drill.

Earlier in the season, there is little doubt this game ends with a Seahawks' field goal to win but not cover the spread but on 'regression' weekend they won 30-20 and covered easily.

One last win on the weekend was a Three-Team Tease of Miami (+3.5) at Indianapolis, Tampa (+7.5) at Oakland and Atlanta (+1.5) at home versus Dallas. I loved this tease because it got me over key numbers on the two road games and pushed Atlanta down to basically just win. On the Miami game I would need every bit of this teased line when the Dolphins lost by three. Tampa made the spread moot by halftime in their domination of the Raiders. Little known fact of gambling: when a rookie running back runs for 250 yards and 4 touchdowns, underdogs of more than a touchdown tend to cover.

With only Atlanta between me and a win, I again hedged the win with a bet on Dallas at +4.5. This is the 3rd time I have hedged a tease with one team left and neither previous time did I end up needing the hedge at all when my team won easily. Based on that, I didn't fully hedge my total bet here, just a portion so it wouldn't be a total loss. If you really think about it, just by teasing the line down I have already hedged it at least partially. Why throw money away hedging a partially hedged bet?

(NOTE: This comment will absolutely come back to bite me at some point in the future).

When Atlanta held a 3-point lead with twenty seconds remaining in the game I actually sat in the creamy middle of winning both bets, what John, Rodney and I have begun referring to as a 'Twinkie.' Unfortunately, after failing to get a first down, the Falcons kicked a chip shot field goal and stretched their lead to six. Twice in using the hedging tactic I have been less than 30 seconds from winning both and failed both times.

Yet, I will continue to follow this approach because it is the mathematically sound approach. If we have learned anything this week: math don't lie.

Sports Infidelity

There is a debate among sociologists, anthropologists and middle-aged businessmen out of town on work trips about the nature of man. Is man meant to be monogamous? Is man really meant to be dedicated to a single partner for their life or are they meant to spread their seed as far and wide as possible to ensure the survival of the species?

The seed spreading theory made a lot of sense when humans spent their days out-running tigers. If you are the slowest and least fierce animal in the jungle, any philosophy that maximizes the chances of your species' survival is a very good thing. Logically, those that spread their seed the furthest were most likely to survive. In this way, the inclination toward infidelity may actually have evolved into being a defining trait of our species – a key component of the natural selection of humans. By this (admittedly wholly unscientific) line of thinking, we today are the children of philanderers. It is literally bred into us.

Note: If you use this chapter as an excuse when your significant other catches you cheating I will NOT be a witness for the prosecution at her subsequent murder trial.

But now, the debate wonders if in a time when the greatest threat to humans is super-sized sodas, should we move past these inherited traits and embrace monogamy?

Cases like John Wayne Bobbit may argue it is now in humanity's interest to be monogamous. Now that other humans have replaced wild animals as the greatest threat to our well-being, the longest surviving humans are more likely to be monogamous. What is that they say about a woman scorned? Exactly.

In a thousand years, in the greatest of ironies, evolution may result in the devout and pious being the only ones that remain – they may end up inheriting the very Earth they expect to leave to the meek – thanks to the natural selection process they disdain as godless mythology.

These broad existential questions derive from an internal debate that has been raging within me for the last few days. However, this debate has nothing to do with the survival of the species, but rather the survival of my bankroll.

I came to Las Vegas to spend six months gambling on football. It is my focus and the sport I know the best. If there is any sport where I have a prayer of turning a profit, it is in football. Yet my eye has started to wonder.

As November turns to December, college football is coming to an end. The point spreads of the NFL are tightening to a point in which it is increasingly hard to find value. Every team has weaknesses and strengths. The old saying of 'any given Sunday…' seems to resonate even more than usual this year (although that is probably subjective, given this is the first season in which I have money riding on games every single weekend). Meanwhile, the NBA and college basketball are both just starting to kick off. In the sheer number of games, could I find more opportunities for value, even if I don't know the sport as well? Should I re-allocate portions of my bankroll from the NFL to NBA or college basketball?

Should I remain faithful to my first love or spread my seed far and wide hoping to ensure survival of my bankroll?

A Thursday night in early November is a good example. I had the Saints in a 3-team tease as ten point underdogs at Atlanta, so despite Drew Brees' best efforts, I gained a push out of the game when the Falcons won 23-13. The Saints were actually one of my favorite picks of the week (at +4, they made my personal LVH SuperContest top five). The Falcons have struggled at home and the Saints were playing for their playoff lives. It just seemed like it would end up being a 3-point game. The Saints had every opportunity to make it a three point game but failed again and again. I was lucky to even get the push on my Tease.

Meanwhile, on the hardcourt, the Nuggets were playing at Golden State and were one point favorites. These two teams are pretty equal, so I avoided the game at the start. But then the Nuggets took a 9-point lead into halftime. Having watched a lot of NBA games over the years it seemed clear that the Warriors would close down that lead in the second half; that is how every NBA game goes. I ended up betting on the Warriors at -2.5 in the second half (meaning if the Nuggets won by less than seven points or the Warriors won, I cashed my bet). Basically, a team that you had to bet as 1-point underdog before the game was now a 6-point underdog. The book was giving 5 free points.

Naturally the Warriors came back (because NBA teams always do), ultimately winning the game by one after the Nuggets' Andre Igoudala hit a three-pointer a millisecond after the final buzzer. I won my bet and was frankly more confident in it than any NFL game this week.

Does this mean that I should abandon the NFL completely to focus on the NBA or college basketball? Not likely. A single anecdotal win doesn't mean anything, as the coming weeks will prove repeatedly.

But let's take a quick checkpoint on the precious bankroll I am so concerned about. College football is over (save Conference Championships and Bowls). NFL is in its final weeks followed by playoffs. My bankroll was based on a worst case scenario of losing consistently which obviously hasn't occurred. Three months into this little experiment and my bankroll is down less than 10%. 90% of the amount I prepared to lose before arriving is still in my bank account.

I can look at this one of three ways:

Be thankful I am ahead and remain conservative in my gambling; resigned to the money lost today and just try to keep what I still have,

Go super aggressive and look to find a way to return to profit or lose it all before the end of the season,

Become moderately more aggressive, be willing to take more risks and try to get back to profit for the season while accepting the possibility of cutting further into my bankroll.

Naturally I am leaning toward #3. I am not reckless enough to just throw money around and there is no point in remaining conservative. Who wants to lock in a 'minor loss'? That makes no sense.

It is time to start raising my bets. Actually past time, I should have been more liberal from the beginning with my bets on the occasions when I was very confident. But that is what happens when you have months of bets in front of you with no corresponding income, it is easy to want to save cash for a rainy day.

So, yes, while I am increasing the size of my bets, I will also look around for the occasional non-football bet to make, similar to the Warriors' bet above. I am not confident enough in basketball betting to bet consistently but I can look for situations where I think I have a chance: where over/unders are too high, a team might be overrated coming off a back-to-back road game or where I would expect things to return to normal after a strange half.

Obviously, this is one of the big differences between wiseguys and me. You can't make a living by only betting on a single sport for six months. By necessity, wiseguys need to find ways to handicap multiple sports. No matter whether they have a lot of personal experience to leverage they need to find a way to find value in every sport.

Geoff Kulesa, a handicapper that runs Wunderdog Sports embodies this ethic. While he spends all autumn handicapping football games and that is where many of his handicapping clients have come from, he has found over time that other sports like WNBA and hockey can actually end up having as much or more value. He may not be a hockey expert or women's basketball expert (because there is no such thing), but football ends in the first week of February. By knowing two other sports, he actually has nearly year round action to handicap. He can track hockey all spring and into summer (you know, in the years where they actually play a season) and that rolls right into the WNBA season, which covers the hot summer months right up until the football season returns.

An added bonus of betting other sports, especially sports like hockey and WNBA is that there is significantly less attention or interest relative to football. Where any value on a football game is attacked relentlessly, with less attention and money on hockey and WNBA, there is more value for those that know what they are doing. Another professional handicapper that Geoff knows actually first gained attention and saw success by betting on the Arena Football League. With little attention, the models he was already applying to NFL could be modified to take advantage of the less precise AFL football point spreads that haven't seen the enormous attention of an NFL weekend.

I most likely won't get to the point where I am betting on hockey or WNBA (and if I do, please call Gambler's Anonymous), but I definitely can occasionally roll the dice on some NBA or college basketball action. Especially as the NFL season winds down.

It takes a while but I will find approaches to use with moderate success in both the NBA and college basketball. In the NBA, I migrate away from betting on teams against the point spread because it can be so arbitrary whether a team covers or not. A six-point underdog can be in a tie game with 30 seconds left, allow one 3-pointer by the favorite and a couple trips to the free throw to stop the clock and it can quickly turn it into a seven-point loss. A bet that was right for the entire game can then lose.

However the Over/Unders seem to be a little more predictable. Not that they are easily beatable but they at least adhere to some level of logic. My approach looks for outliers from the norm, determining why and then deciding if that is valid.

As background, for the most part, NBA totals sit somewhere around 200 points. This makes sense if you think about how frequently NBA games are in the range of 100-100 (or I guess 101-99). My approach is to look at a slate of games and find the games with lines significantly lower or higher than that number. Totals around 180 or 215 are around the limits you will typically see.

Some research of the teams involved, the average number of points they score and allow to be scored as well as their recent performance can provide an indication why that line is so high or low. Then it is time to develop a hypothesis as to whether the teams are likely to not meet expectations. Will the teams that have a low line score more than expected? Will the teams with a high line score less than expected? If a logical argument can be made, then make the bet.

In college basketball I keep it even simpler. Having watched a few games, I heard repeatedly how difficult it is to win on the road in college basketball. Taking that a step further, it therefore must be even harder for a road favorite to win and cover on the road. In a sport with over 300 teams, rather than looking at an entire universe of college basketball games on which I know little, why not narrow the field a little?

I start by looking solely at home underdogs. Of this group, I then research basics of the performance of both them and their opponent. How have they performed at home recently – both straight up and against the spread? How has their opponent performed on the road? In conference play how have they done against common opponents?

Once enough of these factors indicate that a road favorite may be overrated, I shop lines among the casinos and pull the trigger.

Are these approaches as scientific as the systems I employ in betting the NFL? No. But I also keep the amounts smaller and will evolve it over time.

So, yes, my NFL picks remain my main focus – where I dedicate the majority of both my time and money but that doesn't mean I won't look around a little. I don't think the NFL will care about my sending a drink to that sweet-looking basketball game sitting at the bar.

At this point, I will do whatever I can to stay one step ahead of the tiger trying to take all my money.

Conference Championship Weekend

HAWAII (-6) VS SOUTH ALABAMA
This game actually opened at Hawaii -3.5 but was bet up to 6 before I could get the bet down. Oh, to get it at -3.5.

Alas, I still think Hawaii wins handily because this comes down to a game of motivation. If there is ever a game where one team is 'just happy to be there' this is it. This is as close as South Alabama is getting to a bowl after going 2-10 this season. Traveling nearly 7,000 miles to finish your season in a tropical paradise, it is hard to see S. Alabama coming in with much motivation. After a few days on the beach, all the 'win one for the Gipper' speeches can only help so much.

Hawaii on the other hand, is just having another home game; a week after whipping another bad mainland team (UNLV) at home 48-10. The Warriors want to end a bad season on a high note. Dominating two teams at home from two different conferences will do that.

MIDDLE TENNESSEE STATE MONEYLINE (+310) AT ARKANSAS STATE

The rationale for this is pretty easy: have you watched the Sun Belt???

It is madness down there. Every week, the newly perceived favorite gets knocked off. At various points, Florida International, Western Kentucky, Louisiana-Monroe and Louisiana-Lafayette would have been the favorite to win the Sun Belt. Now, MTSU and Ark. St. play to determine who wins the conference. I have no idea whether MTSU can beat Arkansas State but a few things to think about:

1 – Middle Tennessee State went into Atlanta and beat Georgia Tech handily earlier this season

2 – Arkansas State coach Gus Malzahn is on the short list of every open head coach position in the SEC. That list is three schools long now and was four schools long as of a week ago. You are saying he wasn't at least slightly distracted by all this talk?

I'm not saying it is a lock, but at over three times your money, doesn't it seem reasonable that MTSU pulls the upset outright here?

♪♪♪♪

"I think you have spent too much time in Las Vegas. It might be time to go home."

So was the advice of the nice woman in the Oklahoma Sooner shirt that I sat next to for the afternoon games on Saturday.

Sitting in The Sporting House at New York-New York, we were crammed on to a back ledge of the bar area watching the Alabama/ Georgia SEC Championship game when she mentioned this to me. All because I admitted how watching an entire football season in Las Vegas has changed how I enjoy football games.

Remember when ESPN decided to 'leverage their brand by expand- ing into new revenue streams' and opened up ESPNZone bars in most major cities? They offered overpriced food and drink and wall to wall TVs. Having visited at least four or five of these back in the early 2000s I am overly familiar with the concept, so watching games at The Sporting House was a nostalgic trip back for me. When it opened this was ESPNZone Las Vegas, but when the chain was finally shut- tered across much of the country (I honestly don't know if any remain open and don't care enough to research it), this was re-branded The Sporting House.

When I say re-branded I mean just that. Nothing else changed but the words inside the logo. It is a bar/restaurant with three different seat- ing/viewing areas on a main floor and a balcony area (closed the day I was there). This isn't the New York-New York's sportsbook, the ticket window is outside the front, but it is really the place to watch games, eat and drink while watching sports. The sports book has two rows of chairs set behind a small dividing wall separated from the main walk- way connecting NY-NY and Monte Carlo, which feels like it is placed solely as a courtesy – like a dentist's waiting area. The Sporting House is a sports bar. Think of the seating at your local Buffalo Wild Wings or Champps and you get the idea. There was no evidence that the bar could control the outcome of games like at BWW, however, or I would have paid handsomely for Middle Tennessee State to at least put up a fight against Arkansas State.

The SEC title game was an immensely entertaining game, filled with momentum changes and great plays. It was everything that anyone could want from a game between two of the top five teams in the country playing for a shot at the national title. Even with no rooting interest, it was the perfect capper to the season.

But could I strictly enjoy the game? No, because part of my brain was beating itself up for not betting on Georgia even though I liked them as underdogs of more than a touchdown.

Earlier, when I first sat next to this woman, she was lamenting people cheering for TCU against Oklahoma before I had arrived. She stared down the offending parties and noted that they were wearing no TCU colors and therefore she decided they were strictly cheering against OU, not for TCU. She couldn't understand why these people would be so anti-Sooner.

Barring the possibility these were descendants of people forced to walk the Trail of Tears, I set forth the obvious explanation she wasn't seeing. They weren't against Oklahoma out of some unjustified dislike. They had simply bet against them.

In her innocent football fan mind, there were two reasons to cheer for a team: you either like them or loathe their opponent. But in Las Vegas there is a much more likely explanation – money.

It starts as an innocent bet on a game in which you have no vested interest. A way to add another layer of intrigue to the English Trifle that is a college football game. However, spend enough time immersed here and it is no longer a side act. It is the main plot.

After three months of watching football in Las Vegas, I watch games through one of three lenses:

(1) With the stress of a bet on one of the teams involved

(2) With the regret of not betting on a team performing well

(3) With the relief of not betting on a team failing to meet expectations.

Even games involving my favorite teams - when I rarely choose to add money to the already lethal levels of stress I feel during the game - I view through the prism of the betting line.

In attendance at the Florida State /Clemson game in Tallahassee earlier this year, I cringed when Clemson scored a touchdown in the last few moments. Not that the touchdown changed the end result of the game at all, but an 11-point win failed to cover the spread that an 18-point win did. My first thought was 'damn, we didn't cover.' Yet I had no money on the game and should have been focused on the joy of a win over a top ten conference rival.

Spend enough time here and your point of view is irrevocably altered. A simple sporting event is never enough on its own. It is just one aspect of the drama. It is a little like watching *Mr. and Mrs. Smith* now that we know it was the cause of Brad Pitt leaving Jennifer Aniston for Angelina Jolie. Yes, without that knowledge, you can enjoy the movie's plot. But when you watch, understanding the real world of drama simmering underneath, a new layer of complexity is exposed. The movie just looks different.

Yes, it's different, just as watching a football game after a Vegas brainwashing is different. The favored team, Alabama, won an exciting game. But did they win by as much as they were expected to?

Will my brainwashing go away next year when I am not immersed in it every day? Probably. I am sure I will still scan the sports section each week to see where the lines sit but the overriding obsession about it is sure to fade without the immediacy of monetary wins and losses each week.

The question remains, though, as to whether I can enjoy the inherent drama of sport without the added layers of tension. Having spent months buried in this, can I return to the surface and the simple enjoyment of a game for its face value drama or will I find that constantly lacking?

I guess I will find out next year. That wasn't a concern on Saturday. Even though I hadn't bet on the SEC title game, I had money active on plenty of other games.

My two Achilles heels this season have been trying to figure out which Sun Belt team would be better this week and which Big Twelve defense might sort of show up for once. It is only fitting that on the final week of the season I again flex those muscles and again see mixed results.

My Big XII bets involved Oklahoma (-6.5) at TCU and Oklahoma State (-4.5) at Baylor. OU and TCU's back and forth ended with OU holding on to win by seven, 24-17 and squeak out the win for me. Naturally that meant Oklahoma State would play like a bunch of men. Forty-year-old men, that is. Oklahoma State's defense apparently got confused by the new Big XII schedule and assumed their final game was the annual Bedlam contest versus Oklahoma last week. Baylor came out and throttled the Cowboys early and OSU could never recover, losing 41-34. This being the same Baylor team that gave up 70 points to West Virginia.

Random note: The Big XII has ten teams, none of whom play defense. The Big Ten has twelve teams, none of whom play offense. College football is a sick, illogical mind puzzle, built specifically to confuse us.

Shifting down to my old friends in the Sun Belt, I bet on Middle Tennessee State (+11) at Arkansas State. After a season of tracking and betting on the chaos of the Sun Belt, I took a small flyer on one last bit of chaos. Anything and everything happened in the Sun Belt this season, so shouldn't the final game be the encapsulation of that ethic?

I guess, in one sense it was. If the game was expected to be a wild shoot-out, the unexpected would be a one-sided blowout.

45-0, Arkansas State. Well played Red Wolves.

The final bet of the weekend was a fitting sendoff of the season; a bet on Hawaii (-6) at home against South Alabama. Those late night Hawaii games are always one of my favorite college football traditions, so it seemed appropriate to say aloha with one final bet on the Rainbow Warriors.

Sadly, I didn't get to watch this game. Back across the Strip at my 'home' sports book, not even the MGM sports book could find a feed. I was really hoping to send off the college football season by spending one last evening with the local Hawaii broadcasting team, for my money the finest broadcasting duo in the country, but I couldn't. Sorry guys, see you next year.

Instead, I had to track the game on my phone. I don't know what ebbs and flows occurred but it sure seemed like S. Alabama, came out as flat as I expected. A bad team, in their final game trading the Gulf coast for Hawaii, of course they weren't focused and Hawaii cruised to a 23-7 win. But I bet South Alabama enjoyed the luau.

NFL Week #13

HOUSTON (-4.5) AT TENNESSEE

Admittedly, this is almost bragging as much as it is advice. I got this bet down early in the week and this line is now as available as a ticket to a Saints' playoff game. The last line I saw for this game was Houston -6. It is still appealing because I expect the Texans to win by a touchdown, but not quite as appealing – kind of like settling for Maryland as a new member to your conference when you had your heart set on Notre Dame <cough> Big Ten <cough>.

What is there to say to support this pick? The Texans are just better. The Titans come home after an embarrassing loss in Jacksonville, the Texans off an overtime Thanksgiving win in Detroit. Extra rest and motivation to eliminate the doubts starting to creep in after two consecutive overtime wins over mediocre teams should be enough for the Texans to come into this game and dominate.

CAROLINA (-3) AT KANSAS CITY

It is so cute how Las Vegas tries to play soccer mom for the Chiefs – no really, you aren't as bad as it appears! Only a three point underdog at home is cute. It almost seems to imply that the Chiefs have a home field advantage. Unfortunately, that is now just false. On the rare occasion when Chiefs' fans actually make noise now, it is probably just to boo their own players. Or cheer when they get concussed.

The only argument for the Chiefs is that Carolina played on Monday night, so they come in off a short week. Oh ok, I guess the other argument is that the Panthers are still coached by Ron Rivera. But with Romeo Crennel under the headsets for Kansas City, the coaching incompetence is at best a push.

The Chiefs have given up on this season. Last week's loss to the Broncos was the final twitch of the corpse against a division rival. If I only need to lay a field goal against the Chiefs, I will take it all day.

ᔓᔓᔓᔓ

I don't need to watch the Weather Channel every day, as Nick Saban claims, to know that Sunday morning dawned with clouds over every NFL city.

With the shocking, numbing news out of Kansas City that linebacker Javon Belcher had killed his girlfriend and then driven to Chiefs' facilities and committed suicide in front of GM Scott Pioli, and coach Romeo Crennel, it was hard to really get excited about a slate of NFL games.

Yes, the games would be played because if there is one thing Roger Goodell is not hypocritical about, it is his belief that the NFL should always make as much money as possible even if at the expense of things like moral decency. But, in the face of the incomprehensible, can we really get emotionally invested in week #13 of the NFL? What was truly at stake here? Twelve weeks have passed, four weeks still to play. This was truly one of those lost weekends that will be forgotten in a month's time. And yet the games would go on.

In Kansas City, the game kicked off as scheduled and I can't even begin to imagine how the Chiefs prepared to play.

While some people outside the team inflamed the tragedy to make political points, the men that knew Belcher best had to struggle with the loss of a friend while realizing they may have never known him at all. All while preparing to play an NFL game.

I have mocked Romeo Crennel countless times for his poor coaching but I struggle to even imagine what it would be like to watch someone you know kill themselves and then turn around in twenty-four hours and coach an NFL game. How that image doesn't consume you is beyond me.

A young woman was killed. A young man apparently snapped and left a child alone with no parents. Whether it is trying to make a bigger political point or ensuring we leverage our brand to maximize our revenues, sometimes we focus on the broader things at the expense of the small things.

Like a child that will grow up and never understand why her parents are gone.

As always, yes, I bet on the NFL games this week. I won some and I lost some, just like every week. My mood can be dictated by the success of my bets; bets laid on games played in which grown men strap on pads and run into each other. It is silly and ridiculous yet serious business for many.

I had actually laid a bet on Carolina (-3) early in the week but can't say I ever spent much time worrying about it once Sunday came. When I awoke on Sunday morning I texted Turner and Peffer to confirm that we were all in agreement there was little doubt the Chiefs would win – we have seen this enough to know that in the face of tragedy teams invariably find a way to win. As Peffer replied 'if Carolina losing helps bring some healing to Kansas City, it is a worthy sacrifice.' I agree.

Later, walking into the Wynn sports book on Sunday afternoon, it looked like any other NFL Sunday – people cheering and groaning as their teams or bets won and lost. A man in front of me (apparently) won a sizable bet on the Colts' money line and screamed and danced a little jig of joy. He will remember that last second Andrew Luck touchdown for years and tell stories at parties about winning so much money on a touchdown scored on the final play of the game.

He wasn't alone, though. I too got wrapped up in my bets like most either weeks, even achieving something I never thought I would accomplish – the perfect game. Coming off a stinging Bears loss and with nothing left in play during the afternoon slate of games I decided to bet against my heart and on the Buccaneers as 8.5 point underdogs in Denver against my Broncos. This is the first time I have actively bet against one of my favorite teams all season. It was a risky move that was sure to upset some people who would never dare bet against a team for which they cheer. After I admitted the bet, Peffer didn't talk to me the rest of the day and I am pretty sure still looks down on me. The logic was simple – the spread was too big. The Broncos winning at home by 7 against a solid team and still winning my bet sounded like a perfect storm.

When the Bucs took a 3-point lead into half, I was feeling good about the bet. Then the Wynn announced the 2nd half line was Broncos -7, meaning they would cover or push if they won by 4 points or more. This gave me a hedge and window to a Twinkie (the soft, creamy middle of winning two off-setting bets) if the Broncos won by 5 to 8 points.

In the third quarter, the Broncos came out and dominated to take a 28-10 lead into the fourth quarter. My hedge was looking pretty smart. After exchanging field goals to make the score 31-13, my bet on Tampa to lose by eight or less looked done. But the Bucs rallied. Kicking a field goal with under three and a half minutes to play put them only 15 points down. Suddenly, a 'meaningless' touchdown in the closing moment would get me into magic Twinkie land. A three and out by the Broncos gave the Bucs the ball around mid-field. Two completions later, they were inside the ten. And then they scored a touchdown with two and a half to play to make the score 31-23. A failed onside kick and a first down by the Broncos allowed them to finish the game in victory formation, celebrate an eight point win and allowed me to bask in the glow of my finest gambling accomplishment

– winning two bets and having my favorite team win all in the same game.

If I were George Costanza, I would stop betting right here to ensure I go out on top but I can't stop now.

As the NFL has proven, the games stop for nothing.

In-Game Betting

Possibly the greatest invention of the 21st century for football fans who like to watch games from home is the NFL Network's Red Zone Channel. The Red Zone Channel is the Uncle Jesse to the NFL Network's Danny Tanner – they are sort of related but one is just so much cooler.

Only broadcasting on NFL Sundays, the Red Zone Channel is a never-ending whirlwind where a single host bounces what is shown from game to game as teams enter the red zone: possessing the ball inside their opponent's twenty yard line. Their stated goal is to show every single scoring play from a day of NFL action.

In today's ADD-inflicted society, where fans are as concerned or more about their fantasy teams than they are about their actual favorite team, the Red Zone has become the perfect answer to a need few of us consciously realized we had. No longer content to watch the same two teams play for four hours, when the vast majority of the time is spent with little chance of scoring or at commercial, the Red Zone enables us to go where the action is at all times. There is no lingering. No worthless sideline reports. No announcers filling dead space with ludicrous and inane comments. There are just constant scoring chances. One after the other after the other.

The Red Zone channel's popularity could be seen as a negative statement about Americans' ability to focus on and enjoy a single long drawn-out drama – not to mention the statement it makes about our appetite for baseball games – but I look at it in a more positive light. We crave action.

It is this same craving of action that has led to the latest innovation in sports gambling – in-game betting. Exactly what it sounds like, rather than placing bets on a game before kick-off or at the half, in-game betting allows you to bet on the game in real-time. No longer is a bettor forced to place a bet and wait for hours to see if they won or lost. Now, you can win and lose in mere moments.

Just like the Red Zone channel bouncing to a new game after a team misses a field goal there is no dwelling on lost bets here. Regardless of whether the bet is won or lost, the bettor moves on to the next bet in a moment's notice.

While it is now slowly taking over The Strip, the first time I was confronted by in-game betting was about as far away from Las Vegas as you could possibly imagine: India.

In 2005, my job took me to India to work for a couple weeks that coincided with a multi-day series of cricket matches between India and Sri Lanka. My first day in country – a Sunday – as I struggled with jet lag and culture shock, I left the cricket match on my hotel room TV as I dozed off and on all evening. By the time the match had ended and I fell asleep for good, I was just starting to understand the basics of the sport. My elementary school understanding of the sport was broadened over the next few days as I met and worked with a number of locals who lived and died with cricket.

Even one-day matches take hours to complete, so when the series resumed mid-week we were still at the office. Like an American office during March Madness, this led to all of my co-workers pulling up a web-site reporting live scoring and leaving it up in the background on their computers all day. Naturally being the sports junkie that I am, I did the same. As the games reached conclusion, the guys I worked with, myself and about 200 others, made their way to the cafeteria to watch the final Overs on TV (I am not going into the details of cricket. Just think of it sort of like baseball and in this context an Over is an inning).

I am sure there is probably some grand narrative to be woven about how, despite cultural gaps wider than the Grand Canyon, a passion for sport is clearly a human condition inherent to us all. Like that movie, Babel, except with sports instead of death being the unifying trait. I, however, am not that smart. Instead, the impression that was left was how advanced the cricket world was in gambling.

In addition to constantly tracking the score, Overs and wickets remaining (seriously, Google it, it makes a lot more sense than American football), the web site we were watching also had a small box off to the side that showed betting odds constantly updated. You could bet on the number of runs scored in the next Over (six pitches), number of runs scored by an individual batter, total runs scored by a side, etc. All in real time. All from the comfort of your desk - though I don't think gambling on a work computer, during the workday would be the best decision career-wise.

I guess, in hindsight, that it makes sense India would lead the way in sports gambling. A tech-savvy country, with historic ties to England, one of the most gambling-friendly countries on Earth and enraptured by a sport that takes, literally, days to complete in its most basic form; of course, they would look for a way to enliven the proceedings with gambling. If we think that placing a bet that takes four hours for resolution is too slow, imagine what it would be like to have to wait days to see if your bet won.

Given that glimpse of the possibilities (I didn't actually participate), it was a long wait to be able to do the same here stateside. But I finally succumbed.

There are two companies here in Las Vegas that have developed on-line gambling applications that also allow for real time in-game gambling. One is William Hill U.S., the local subsidiary of the king of English betting houses. The other is Cantor Gaming, an offshoot of Cantor Fitzgerald, the large financial services company. Cantor runs the sports books of several casinos in Las Vegas (Cosmopolitan, Venetian, Palazzo, Palms and Hard Rock to name a few). William Hill manages the sportsbooks at dozens of small casinos and betting parlors scattered throughout Nevada.

Thankfully, for the sake of my bankroll, I didn't begin exploring in-game betting until much of the season was already gone. Had I spent every Saturday and Sunday of the season with access to in-game betting options, I would likely be significantly poorer today. It wasn't until December that I signed up for a Cantor account.

Three options exist for partaking of the in-game betting with Cantor. You can use one of the many computers that line the Cantor sports books; you can load the application on to a personal computer or you can load it on to a mobile device. To answer the obvious question, you also must download a location validator application on to your mobile device that ensures you are trying to use the device in the state of Nevada (you know, the only state with legal sports gambling).

Once you access the application, you select which games you wish to follow, watch the odds change in real time, and place bets (debiting from the investment you put into your account when opening it). For the vast majority of games, the options available on the application are the same available in any sports book – money line, point spread and over/under lines for full games and first halves.

However, for a few select games (on NFL weekends it is one to two within each of the morning and afternoon sessions), the betting options become greatly expanded. Lines are posted for over/unders on the total yardage of quarterbacks, running backs or wide receivers. The full game point spread and over/under adjust throughout the game to reflect the current score. For some offensive drives, odds will be posted on whether a first down will be achieved as well as how the drive ultimately ends (punt, field goal attempt, touchdown, turnover). Odds reflect the action coming in and the flow of the game.

Frankly, for anyone with the gambling gene, in-game can be dangerously seductive. Like seeing a beautiful woman smiling at you across the room at some swanky cocktail party, you can quickly be enraptured and before you know what you are doing, you are giving away every penny to your name.

The 'beautiful woman' part of the previous analogy may be conjecture based on watching too many spy movies, but it is undoubtedly true of in-game betting.

Faced with so many options at your fingertips, many of which have incredibly alluring odds and very low minimums it is easy to get out of control. The betting options for a field goal attempt or scoring a touchdown on a drive are often at +300 or higher. Soon enough, your experience becomes something like:

What could it hurt to throw $5 on the offense scoring here, I can make three times my money! <PUNT>

Ok, they didn't score last drive, but they will this dri<PUNT>

This offense is due they will defi<INTERCEPTION>

SONOFA<FUMBLE>

Outside of applying balm to your ADHD, and making it somehow profitable to wager on the Cardinals' offense, real time betting does actually have a value to gamblers. The best way to take advantage of in-game betting isn't to try to guess what happens on a single drive, it is to project the end of the game based on what you have already seen. As mentioned, in addition to the individual drive bets, in-game provides a constant stream of in-game updates to the point spread and over/under line. A lot of early scoring and the over/under can sky-rocket. One team jumps out to a big lead and the point spread will move. The opportunities exist when you think the action to date isn't indicative of the remainder of the game so you take advantage of momentary gaps in the spread.

Two high-scoring teams start out slow and the over/under falls rapidly. If you believe they will rally and ultimately score near original expectations you can bet the Over. An underdog jumps out early on a favorite? Bet on the favorite at artificially low spreads. You may still be wrong, that is why they call it gambling, but there are typically a few windows where real value can be found. We have all watched enough football to recognize that even if a big road underdog jumps out to a lead, they are unlikely to keep it. But in the moments that immediately follow such a score, the casinos have to adjust the line and if you truly believe that the pre-game expectations are more accurate than what just happened, there are opportunities.

Before in-game betting arrived, the only way to bet after a game kicked off was at halftime. Now with in-game betting you can capitalize at the moment something happens that significantly changes the odds. You can hedge pre-game bets or just take advantage of something that differs from what you expect.

In-game betting is the next big thing in Las Vegas, I would expect more of the bigger sportsbook companies to produce their own mobile applications and real time betting soon. Yet the irony is that in-game

betting actually hearkens directly back to gambling's humble begin-
nings – sitting in baseball bleachers early in the 20th century betting
on the outcome of individual at-bats.

And for me, it will always take part of me back to a cubicle in
Bangalore, India.

Week #14

ARMY VS NAVY UNDER (56.5 POINTS)
*Some might argue it is un-American to gamble on the Army vs Navy
game. It is wrong to wager on the outcome of a contest between two
teams made up of the finest men our country can produce; teams of
incredibly intelligent, hardworking men willing to make sacrifices few of
us would. Many could have gone to fancy schools and earned high paying careers but instead they are going through four of the hardest years
a teenager could imagine with the only reward at the other end of the
tunnel being possibly a life of constant danger and unimaginable horrors.
It cheapens what these men do by attempting to profit from their efforts.*

*In reality, gambling on this game is not an affront to their sacrifice but
a celebration of it. In my lifetime our capitalist society has fought cold
and hot wars against communists and religious fanatics that see our
decadent way of life as an outrage to their equally corrupt ideologies.
What better way to raise a middle finger to those that disparage the
'western way of life' than to both celebrate our military heroes while
at the same time making a little money on them. That is as American
as anything in this country not named Brett Favre.*

*I am taking the Under here because (1) these teams haven't hit the
Over in their last six meetings and this line is higher than all but one
of those lines that they didn't hit and (2) I may make money off our
Armed Services but I am not going to pick one over the other. I believe in all Armed Services equally not scoring a lot of points.*

As Gerald Ford said: "A strong defense is the surest way to peace."

I am sure 'and winning bets' is implied.

NEW ENGLAND (-3.5) VS HOUSTON

As disappointing as it is to have almost no college football this week-end, it is even worse that the NFL games aren't really appealing. Either very large spreads or close spreads in which it feels like a coin flip is the difference between the two. I like Indy at home -5 versus Tennessee, but have had some bad experiences in similar situations betting against the Titans (see: at Buffalo and at Jacksonville).

Instead I will go with the most public bet of them all – the Patriots. I tend to think the Pats are overrated by Vegas (7-5 season to date against the spread), but not this week. The Pats seem to get a little lazy and sloppy against inferior teams but at home, on national TV against the AFC team with the best record I think they come out and make a statement. Houston is still getting used to this 'hunted' tag and I don't think they are quite ready for it. They got crushed by the Packers at home on a Sunday night earlier this year, a team structur-ally similar to the Pats in the reliance on a strong passing game and a defense with holes. The Pats, meanwhile, play their best against the best teams – look at what they did to the Broncos, a dominating win that looks much more impressive today than it did at the time.

If there is one bet I wish I could make on this game it is the Over on the number of times Jon Gruden uses the phrase 'this guy' during the broadcast. Between Tom Brady, Arian Foster, Aaron Hernandez, Wes Welker, Andre Johnson and J.J. Watt, the 'this guy' over/under line would need to be higher than a line for a re-match of the 70-63 West Virginia/Baylor game. That Over would be Super Double Lock of the Century.

Fittingly for a city that has built an advertising campaign around the theme of 'what happens here, stays here', Las Vegas has a secret. It may not be obvious to a visitor here for a few days of drunken debauchery but the longer you stay here, the more obvious it becomes.

Las Vegas is an optical illusion.

Everything about the city is not what it seems to be. From the simple fact that the size of the casinos makes everything appear closer than it actually is to the illusion of glamour that permeates every casino, it is all a lie built to entice.

The Las Vegas of advertisements is pulled directly from an episode of Keeping Up with the Kardashians or Entourage – glamorous people having the time of their lives. But in reality, it is desperate people- -people extending themselves beyond what they can afford chasing that image. Whether it is losing money at casino tables or squeezing into a dress three sizes too small and paying $20 per drink in a club, Las Vegas makes people believe they are living in a fantasy world for a few days. It is only when you pick up your head and look around that you see the people around you aren't models (Assuming you are still sober enough to tell).

There are no clocks and no windows in casinos for a reason – partially to keep you gambling long past when you should and partially to reinforce the belief that this fantasy world in which you are living is wholly distinct from the regular world outside. Back at home you can't afford to lose $500 in two hours of playing craps. In here you can, because this isn't the real world, it is more like a movie.

Of course, if you do escape the casinos, reality provides an ugly reminder of its existence. Not more than two blocks off the Strip sit old, worn down apartments housing people that came here chasing one dream and ended up living another.

I have now been here three months. Las Vegas is no longer a dream land of endless wonders for me. It is just where I live. I am staying right on the Strip but spend more time away from the Strip – whether shopping for groceries or working on these pages at a coffee shop – than I do in those palaces that have come to define VEGAS (all caps and dropping the 'Las' intended).

But still, I had forgotten Las Vegas' other secret. Walking the end-less expanse of the Strip it is easy to imagine those massive casinos stretching as long and as wide as Manhattan. In reality Las Vegas is still just an oasis in the desert. It isn't a never-ending metropolis. It is a small city surrounded by hundreds of miles of mountains and desert.

So, on my first Saturday 'off' since arriving, I decided it was time to re-acquaint myself with actual nature. Twenty minutes after depart-ing the Strip – less time than I need to get to a hiking area back in Denver-I arrived at Red Rock Canyon. An hour and a half later, after a run through the scrub brush sitting at the base of the mountains ringing the Las Vegas valley, I had lungs full of non-recycled air and I was reminded how small the Strip really is. Immersed in it, it can be all-consuming. But seen from a distance it is just a string of buildings, no different than any major city in the country.

Las Vegas isn't some magic wonderland where all responsibilities dis-appear and dreams come true; it is just a city selling an image like Hollywood or 'the city that never sleeps.'

Every time I walk to the sports book in the MGM, I walk by David Copperfield's theater and the bust of Copperfield that appears to have been sculpted by the blind girl from Lionel Richie's video for 'Hello.' I guess if MGM is willing to create a bust of you, you are probably a pretty good magician. Especially if you somehow also convinced a supermodel to marry you.

Fitting then that the couple ultimately broke up before marrying, citing their busy schedules. In Las Vegas, even for legendary magicians, the reality never matches the illusion.

I returned from my run just as the Army vs. Navy game was ending. As mentioned above, there was a strong history of these teams failing to cover the Over/Under line in recent years, so I bet the Under (56 points). These teams end up giving up a lot of points during the season to teams full of players dreaming of the NFL and score points on those same teams by employing the novelty of the triple option attack. But when playing each other, it is like playing their own mirror image –or like WOPR playing Thermo-Nuclear War against itself in War Games. There are no tricks because the other team spends all season practicing against a triple option. Both teams are filled with players who have more important things to worry about than the NFL draft. This equality leads to a stalemate. Close, low-scoring games decided by one ill-timed turnover.

Sure enough, Navy led Army 17-13 with only a few minutes to play. Army got inside of Navy's ten yard line before a muffed hand-off resulted in a fumble and a Navy win. Regardless of whether Army had held on to the ball, my bet was won long before.

After a Saturday spent enjoying sunshine and fresh air, I returned to the confines of the sportsbook for my NFL Sunday, with the only difference being I tried a new space, taking a week off from the LVH. This week was spent at the Hard Rock, popping the cherry of my new in-game betting toy. Hard Rock is a Cantor sportsbook and Cantor has built a consistent theme across all of their sports books – wall to wall rows of individual desks with individual TVs and soft chairs, all ensconced in bright red casing.

Each of the TVs allows for a bettor to log into their account and make bets by pressing a couple buttons. You can also segment your personal screen – putting a game in one corner, in-game betting on another and games like video poker on another corner. Have ADD and a gambling problem? A Cantor casino is the place for you.

Set off to the side of the main casino floor behind glass walls, Hard Rock's sports book has 4-5 rows of these seats facing a large wall of TVs, with a betting desk underneath it. The bet boards are to the side and behind the rows of TVs. It is small, compact, efficient, sleek and modern. It is like the Fiat of sports books.

The front wall is covered by HD TVs from wall to wall. Given its compact size, watching the games requires a relatively steep look up the wall, especially in the first couple rows, but the chairs rock back fairly deeply so you don't end up craning your neck all day. The bet boards being set to the side and behind require you to swivel to see lines on the boards themselves, but the same information is found on your individual cubbie TV if you know how to navigate it.

Earlier in the week, I had put $500 in my Cantor account (then immediately borrowed against it to place a losing bet on Manny Pacquiao). After finding a seat at one of the long rows of red lacquered desks and with a morning slate of games that I didn't care about, I logged into my account and started placing small in-game bets. Here is an actual list of my first real time bets from that morning and their outcomes:

1. San Diego to finish the drive with a field goal attempt against Pittsburgh (+243) – Loss

2. Cincinnati to finish the drive with a field attempt against Dallas (+325) – Loss

3. Cincinnati to score a touchdown on drive (+255) – Loss

4. Cincinnati to finish the drive with a field goal attempt against San Diego (+117) – Loss

5. Steelers to rally from a deficit and defeat San Diego (+117) – Loss

Things turned around in the afternoon, when the Cardinals played Seattle and turned over the ball on nearly every other drive (not hyperbole: the Cardinals ended the day with no points, 6 punts...and 8 turnovers). With turnovers consistently posted at over +300 odds, you could place a bet on this and combine it with 'No First Down achieved' (at around +200) every single drive and easily win more than you bet.

In between betting on the Cardinals best Three Stooges impression, I also bet on the Forty-Niners against the Dolphins. Prior to the game, the Forty-Niners were prohibitive favorites, with the point spread hanging around 10 points and an Over/Under of 38.5. However, both offenses started slowly and at the half the Niners led only 6-3. Believing that the Niners had to re-group in the 2nd half and that the offenses would find new plans in the 2nd half, I bet on the Niners at –7.5 and took an Over when the Over/Under line fell all the way to 31.5.

Sure enough, the Niners rallied and held a 7-point lead at 20-13 until San Francisco quarterback, Colin Kaepernick, rolled around the corner and out-raced the Dolphin defense for a 50-yard touchdown a 27-13 lead and a 14-point Niner win that won both my adjusted spread and over/under bets.

My final bets of the day, were placed with my Forty-Niner winning as I walked out. I put some money on the Sunday night game, betting on Detroit (+3.5) in the first half at Green Bay and the Under (48) across the whole game. I haven't had much success betting Sunday night games when the bets are placed at the end of a long day trying to win back losses from earlier but I felt good about these.

The Lions have come out strong in recent weeks against Green Bay and Houston so getting them as an underdog of more than a field goal seemed like a lot of value to me (especially with a pay out of even money). More importantly, the cold, snowy weather in Green Bay seemed to imply to me that we would see a low-scoring, close game between two pass-happy teams that know each other well. Sure enough the Lions' first drive was a seven and a half minute long touchdown drive. My only regret at that moment was not betting more on the first half bet. Ultimately the Lions took a 4-point lead into half, paying my first bet.

In the second half, the Packers rallied and shut down the Lions' offense. Facing a 10-point deficit with less than a minute to play the Lions were deep in the Packers end. Needing two scores, rather than burning a lot of clock seeking a touchdown, they kicked a field goal and then tried for the on-side kick. They failed to recover the on-side kick, and the Packers won 27-20. After the field goal the total settled at 47. Just enough under the 48 I had bet.

My bets had remained relatively small on Sunday because I was all in on the Patriots (-3.5) against the Texans. This was the single largest bet I have laid since I arrived. Part of that derived from a conscious effort to increase the size of my bets; part of it was my absolute conviction that this was the type of game that the Patriots live for: home game against another high powered team, a chance to make a statement. Of course the Patriots were going to win easily. We have seen this game so many times that I was never even considering placing a hedge bet on the Texans even as the spread slid toward Patriots -6. Thankfully I didn't hedge as the Patriots jumped out to a 21-0 lead and won easily 42-14.

The Patriots have been so consistently strong for so long, we have seen all of the storylines at this point. We know exactly what to expect from Belichick and Brady: dominating victories over other quality teams in the regular season--close games against overwhelmed teams that they should dominate. Then inexplicable losses in the playoffs or Super Bowl. The script for the Patriots' season is more repetitive than The Bachelor.

It may be predictable and a little boring having the same Patriots story every season but at least we can profit from its unoriginality.

The System Revisited

It is now about twelve weeks into my little experiment and time to take a step back and evaluate how things have gone to date. My bankroll is down about 10%. After a couple very cold weeks where I couldn't win a thing, I have settled into a disappointing but relatively consistent rhythm of winning a few but losing a few more each week. Ill-advised, impromptu bets, as either attempts to rebound from losses or build on wins, is a constant drag on my winnings.

As the college football season comes to an end, both my writing and handicapping activities get cut in half, so it is time to revisit the system I have employed and maybe see if the experts actually have a better approach than I do. Can't imagine they do, but I guess I should check.

My initial system of leveraging Football Outsiders' DVOA formula to create a power ranking and then compare to the spread, has seen mixed results. Overall in NFL weeks #3 – 13, the system has been right 55.4% of the time (87 correct, 70 incorrect), so equal wagers on every single game would show a small profit (after the Vig). Unfortunately, I have not been betting every game with equal amounts. Instead I have focused on a short list of games that I deem as best bets, as well as last minute capricious bets I talk myself into like grabbing a pack of gum in the check-out line at the store. My NFL bets, therefore, have a record of 23-34 (40%).

Varying the amount of my bets based on my personal confidence has helped me limit my losses to 13% of my total dollars bet in this period (40% win rate on equal sized bets would result in loss of over 23%) but my approach to date has become a recipe for losses slightly more than wins, which is not going to keep me in food and beer for long.

But there are a few weeks left so I have time to see if there is a better way.

Correction – there is definitely a better way, so with a few weeks left, I have time to find it.

It is 2012; there is a world of information at my fingertips so I start where anyone outside of China would start – with a Google search. I guess I could have asked on Twitter or posted on Facebook, but outside of a good recipe for banana bread or the best place to grab a cocktail in South Beach, my Facebook friends wouldn't be much help. Google, however, is.

A few short clicks later, after wading through several tout sites more than happy to allow me to use their systems (for a nominal fee) that are GUARANTEED TO WIN BIG EVERY TIME!!! I finally stumble on a couple articles with the basics of football handicapping systems. One strikes me as being manageable from a weekly effort perspective and logical in its simplicity. And it even has a cool name: The Dudley Method. I am unable to confirm if it is named after Arnold's friend that almost got molested on Diff'rent Strokes but if it was, we can all agree that would be weird.

In summary, the Dudley Method comes down to this – comparing how many yards an offense consumes on average to score a point (points per game/yards per game) relative to how many yards the opposing defense gives up. Complete an analysis for two teams facing each other and you have a projected final score which you can compare to the spread. Biggest differences between point spread and Dudley Method output (adjusted for home field advantage) is your best bet. Rather than developing a power ranking of 1 through 32, this system is all about the weekly match-up – what would we expect Team A's offense to score on Team B's defense and vice versa.

Having a healthy American male ego, though, I can't just take someone else's system as my own – I need to tinker. The Dudley Method description that I read recommends using each team's performance in the previous four games for the basis of your calculations. Yawn. While it gives a good approximation of how that team is performing, those performances are also driven by who they played. If their last four games were against the Jaguars, Jets, Titans and Chiefs (people of the future: in 2012, all these teams were dreadful) while their next game is against the Broncos (very good, obviously) then, as they say in Mutual Fund commercials: past performance is not indicative of future returns.

Since I already have the power ranking of every team – as a whole and of component offenses and defenses – as represented by Football Outsiders DVOA, I decide to refine the Dudley Method: the Modified Dudley or the Mod-Dud if you prefer. I simply find the four games each team has played against teams that most closely resemble the offense and defense they face this week and use their performance in that game. As a tie-breaker of multiple similar opponents, most recent game wins.

I wish I could say that in the first week employing this, I picked every game correctly but no system is perfect. Of the four games it is most confident in, it went 3 for 4. However it missed the next two. But, in all, it goes 11-5, a remarkably good week against the spread. While that performance isn't necessarily sustainable its value is in finding games where a team that doesn't really pass an eye test may be poised for an upset. Carolina, an up and down team I had long ago given up on trusting was a 3-point underdog at San Diego. The Mod-Dud (kinda catchy) said Carolina was 2.5 points better than San Diego, in San Diego, yet the Chargers were favored by 3. The Panthers ended up winning 31-7.

Of course, me being me, one of my biggest bets of the weekend involved that one team of the four highly rated teams that failed. That was the Giants and they got creamed by the Falcons, not even covering a teased line I bet. Those two losses on that one team offset all of the goodness the Mod-Dud bestowed on me.

So my system isn't perfect but it is a step in the right direction. I may not be able to make a living using it, but I won't end up in a roadside ditch either. However, I return to a question I was unable to answer earlier this season: what would a system look like that is actually used to make a living by?

Geoff Kulesa runs Wunderdog Sports, an online handicapping web site. He also happens to live outside Denver and enjoys a good craft beer, so while the Lions played the Falcons on a Saturday evening before Christmas, Geoff and I got together to have a beer and a burger and talk about what he does relative to what I have been doing this fall.

Geoff actually employs a completely different system than anything I have described here. Power rankings, offensive efficiency, pffft. This probably explains how he has turned what was once a hobby in the hours outside of a corporate career into a vocation (which sounds eerily familiar). His approach doesn't mimic others and try to just improve or change the same approach taken by everyone else. Rather he turns the handicapping upside down by ignoring the teams playing altogether.

I can relate to his system because he has actually quantified the anecdotal approach I have always taken to looking at games. My world philosophy has been shaped by the phrases "those that don't understand the past are destined to repeat it" and "I am from Missouri, you have to show me," which makes it convenient because I actually am from Missouri (at least technically – I was born at a hospital on the east side of the Missouri river before returning to my family home at the time outside Kansas City in Kansas).

These phrases basically summarized mean that until I see something that makes this situation different, I am going to assume that it will follow the same pattern I have seen before.

Geoff has taken this same philosophy and uses the massive amounts of data available today to create a system in which he looks at situations to see if there is a discernible betting advantage to be gained. If a team averages two sacks more per game than their opponent, does that correlate to success? If a team got blown out on the road last week, how might they be expected to play at home this week?

His approach isn't about the name on the front of the uniform, or even the name on the back of the uniform. It isn't about the X's and O's or the Jims and Joes. It is about finding teams that, based on some current situation, can be predicted to out-play their expectations.

I am writing this at the beginning of January so this will look either brilliant or hilarious by the time you read this, but when I say I anecdotally use Geoff's system without all of that inconvenient quantification and scientific rigor, here is a perfect example. I love Notre Dame as a big underdog against Alabama in the BCS title game next week. I like Notre Dame solely because of the history of big underdogs with solid defenses keeping games close or winning outright in BCS championship games. The 2006 Florida Gators. The 2002 Ohio State Buckeyes. Even the, gulp, 2000 Oklahoma Sooners against my Noles. All were big underdogs that defied the experts by taking out the high powered team across the line of scrimmage.

Of course, the Wunderdog system requires copious amounts of data and the time to test hypotheses against that data, not something available to the average, casual bettor. But it is nice to know that while I will never be a true professional, I am on the right path.

Week #15

HOUSTON (-8.5) VS INDIANAPOLIS

I hate big point spread favorites. I hate a team winning comfortably, giving up a late meaningless touchdown and winning by seven but losing my bet. I have made a point of almost never betting on big NFL favorites, unless I tease them down to a more manageable number.

But I am breaking with that tradition today because I think this number isn't high enough. Houston is coming off an embarrassing Monday night loss at New England. A loss so bad that there are now doubters wondering if Houston's great record was built on the backs of a schedule as weak as an SEC team's non-conference schedule. I think Houston comes out and makes a statement against a young Colts team that has at times struggled on the road – losing badly at the Bears, Jets and Patriots this year.

Houston may very well be overrated and will be exposed when they meet the Broncos or Patriots again in the playoffs. But this week, they come out and remind us how they got that great record in the first place.

OAKLAND (-3) VS KANSAS CITY

I don't know why I keep coming back to these teams. They are more bi-polar than the roommate from Single White Female. Both teams have shown small flashes of competence yet the vast majority of their records show them as possibly the two worst teams in the league.

But, at least the Raiders losses are mostly self-inflicted. Turnovers and penalties are what have repeatedly killed the Raiders. The Chiefs, however, are just not very good. Bad quarterback play. Little talent but one running back who spends most of each game running for his life. A porous defense.

The Raiders playing at home after a 10-day layoff (following last Thursday's loss to the Broncos) should be more than enough to win this game easily.

A bookmaker that has lived in Las Vegas as long as I have been alive told me, "I still learn something new every day." A pro handicapper told me "when you stop learning and adapting, you need to stop gambling." Given the insight by more knowledgeable and experienced men than me, I shouldn't be surprised that even in week fifteen of this little experiment, I am still learning new things. Yet, I did. I learned the dangers that can be faced by giving in to laziness.

Sometimes, sloth wins out. Sunday morning, I just couldn't get up and going. For the first time since a really bad weekend a couple months ago (read: HANGOVER), I never made it out of my condo and to a sports book to watch games. I just didn't have the motivation and didn't feel the urgency to be anywhere. The Giants can probably relate since they didn't do anything Sunday morning either.

So, I ended up on my couch all day, watching games. I didn't forsake my sacred gambling duty completely, though. My work ethic is too strong for that.

After opening a gambling account while at the Hard Rock last week, I downloaded the Cantor Gaming app to my phone though, strangely, my virus protection blocked me from downloading it on to my computer. Don't judge me, Norton.

Rather than getting in my car and heading to a sports book or even just walking down to MGM, I was able to sit on my couch, watch a game on my TV, track other games on my computer and place bets on my phone. Welcome to 21st century sports gambling – a man too lazy to leave his couch can now watch, track and bet games at the same time.

While the Cantor interface can be a little slow and clunky on a cell phone network using cell service (I also downloaded it on to my iPod Touch using my condo wi-fi, where it works significantly better) when it works it works almost too well.

Sure, I won my first bet when the Seahawks held Buffalo to a three and out to start the game but then I lost bets on the Bills not covering a 16.5 spread after falling behind by 14, and Kansas City not outscoring the Raiders in the 2nd half (despite the Raiders scoring only 6 points and the Chiefs getting inside the ten yard line). Thankfully I finished the day with a win – a small bet parlaying the Niners (+3) and the Under (23.5) in the first half at New England, so it wasn't a total loss.

But beyond any wins and losses, the biggest take-away from this real time, remote gambling experiment is a lesson I already knew deep in my brain; this is just way too convenient for my own good.

Before moving here, I always refused to open an online gambling account, despite this limiting my gambling to annual trips to Vegas. Partially this derives from its illegality, even as ridiculous as that very illegality is. But more importantly, I just don't trust myself with the convenience of it. Being fundamentally lazy, but fostering a minor gambling addiction, the ability to sit on my couch and place bet after bet is dangerous. If that was just theory before this weekend it is now established fact. If I can never even leave my couch on a beautiful mid-December Sunday in Las Vegas and still lose money, What would happen if I were at home in Denver and a blizzard was raging outside? Nothing good, I am sure.

But my gambling education wasn't limited to my in-game betting, it started with the bets I laid during the week. The bet laid on Houston (-8.5) against Indianapolis ended up being a fascinating example of the impact of shopping around for point spreads. I went to the LVH on Friday afternoon to place my SuperContest picks and lay a few bets. Before leaving my computer I checked donbest.com to compare the lines between LVH and MGM and noticed that LVH was significantly higher for this game. Sure enough, when I arrived, LVH had this posted at Houston - 9.5. I decided not to bet on Houston and hope the line hadn't moved at MGM by the time I returned later that evening after a few other errands. As discussed above, I am lazy, so I didn't want to add a 30-minute round trip walk to my evening but decided it might be worth it. MGM still had Houston as only an 8.5 point favorite.

Ultimately the Texans won by 12 so all of this angst and effort didn't matter. But it almost meant everything. Houston took a 26-17 lead with about eight and a half minutes to play in the game. After holding the Colts to a punt the Texans took the ball back over with less than five minutes to play. If they could run out the clock with no more scores, they would win by nine – making the MGM bet a winner and the LVH bet a loser. While somewhere someone was pleading with the Texans to march down and score again, I was left only cheering for the clock. All of that pleading by the other imaginary gambler was rewarded when a series of runs by Arian Foster gashed the Colts defense and resulted in a field goal with a minute to play, providing the final margin of victory, 29-17. Sure, either bet ultimately won but mine was a lot less stressful.

My big afternoon bet proved that after a long enough season even the most unpredictable of teams can occasionally be predictable. If you think about it, whether a team is good or bad really has little to do with their usefulness in sports gambling. It seems paradoxical –like you would want to bet on good teams and bet against bad teams. But that isn't necessarily the case. It is easy to spot a good team – everyone knows what a good team looks like (they have a good record). Thus, point spreads are adjusted accordingly. Understanding who is good or bad isn't important. But understanding who is consistent is important.

The Chiefs and the Raiders are the perfect examples of this. Both are bad teams. It is hard to watch either team and make a legitimate argument that there are aspects of either team that are good. But there is one key difference – the Chiefs are consistently bad. The Raiders are inconsistently bad.

The Raiders have occasionally shown signs of life but there is no pattern or rhythm to when they decide to show up and play well. They take the Falcons to the wire in Atlanta and get destroyed in Baltimore. They beat the Steelers and then lose to Cleveland, both in Oakland.

The Chiefs on the other hand have been predictably, consistently dreadful all season. Outside of the emotional win over the Panthers a couple weeks ago and the still inexplicable win at New Orleans early this year, the Chiefs are the most reliable team in the league – they consistently stink. That is what made this an easy bet to me. The Chiefs weren't going to show up and surprise by playing really well. The only question was whether the Raiders would do enough to take advantage. Five field goals to win 15-0, by definition, is doing just enough to take advantage.

Of course, even knowing all this, I couldn't ignore my in-game options a cell phone away. I put a bet on the Chiefs in the 2nd half that gave me a chance at a Twinkie but ultimately ended up just digging into my profits. The temptation of betting is just too great, even sitting at home. Actually maybe even more acute at home alone with no distractions to keep me from betting. If betting on Brady Quinn seemed like a reasonable idea to me, clearly I can't be trusted.

Next weekend, no matter how lazy I feel, I am definitely going to force myself to go somewhere.

The Bowls

The college football bowl system may be the strangest season finale of any popular sport in the world. In no other sport is a team 'rewarded' for a moderately successful season by playing an exhibition game with no consequences. Even the advent of the college football playoffs in 2014 doesn't change that the vast majority of college football teams with a winning record will finish their season playing a game at a location and against a team with which they have no historic relationship. By any logical approach it makes no sense: "Congratulations on your successful season. Here is a completely random game to play."

While the rest of the world is nowhere near as obsessed as Americans with completing a playoff – see international soccer leagues where a season long competition, in which every game contributes to a cumulative point total (3 points for win, 1 point for tie, 0 points for loss) defines the winner of the league – there is no popular sport where the season ends with a meaningless exhibition. Unless you count the World Series when the Yankees or Red Sox aren't involved.

This is not a criticism of the bowl system. Setting aside the atrocious financial impact of forcing these schools to make ticket guarantees to these incredibly corrupt bowls, I love the bowls. Many of my warmest sport-watching memories of a child are the Bowl games. No childhood memory – not Thanksgiving, Christmas or a birthday

– possesses as warm a spot in my memory as New Year's Days of my childhood.

Living in the Mountain Time zone, by the time I woke up on New Year's morning, I only had to endure an hour or two of the Rose Parade before the first of the Florida bowl games would be kicking off. The Florida games would be followed by the Cotton Bowl, then Fiesta Bowl, then Rose Bowl and finally a nightcap double-header of Orange and Sugar Bowls. All in a single day, rather than the week and a half they require now. My family would lay dime bets on each game (no point spreads though; which in hindsight is kind of embarrassing) and lay out a buffet of completely unhealthy foods to be grazed on all day long. It was a day of gluttony to start the New Year, and quite literally meant the remainder of the year was all downhill from there.

Back when laying those dime bets were the extent of my gambling interests, I didn't realize what the Bowl games really entailed – handicapping games of unequal teams in terms of talent, motivation and preparation. In short, betting bowl games presents a completely new set of challenges from other gambling.

With a month between the end of the season and the start of the bowls, any number of factors can impact how a game plays out. A team can feel slighted by playing in a bowl they view as 'beneath' them. A team can be motivated to prove they belong among the elite. They can spend that month improving; taking time to refocus on the little things that get lost during a long season while also refining their game plan to their opponent. Or they can spend that month regretting mistakes made during the season, losing motivation and interest in playing a game.

I would suggest no sport requires the consideration of intangibles like handicapping the bowl games. Trying to get into the head of a group of nineteen to twenty-two year olds, not to mention their coaches, could drive someone insane.

Unlike developing systems across a broad season, where a complex spider web of performance against common opponents can help project a match-up, a bowl game often brings together two teams of very different experiences, skills and motivations. Projecting how that will result can be significantly harder. Even for these, though, there are some basic guidelines to improve the odds of winning.

#1 – Underdogs Early/Favorites Late

Two separate studies of historical data has shown a consistent theme – underdogs out-perform in December and favorites outperform in January. This would seem to make sense for a couple reasons. The December games involve teams with worse records, or small conference schools facing mediocre large conference teams. Projecting which of these teams is better can be more difficult with little ability to compare their schedules; the point spread may just be wrong. This is also the time when the vast majority of disappointing major teams play. If you are a traditional power playing in December you have probably not met your team goals and are playing with less enthusiasm, often against an opponent relishing a chance to knock off a big name school.

In January, the situation is reversed: most games feature two highly ranked teams who have received considerable attention all season and attention means smarter point spreads. There is also smaller chance that a team will show up unmotivated and unprepared for a marquee January bowl game. They are likely playing an opponent they respect and on a big enough stage that there is no feeling of disrespect to overcome. You may disagree based on high profile upsets, but the occasional Boise State over Oklahoma Fiesta Bowl, West Virginia over Oklahoma Fiesta Bowl or Utah over Alabama Sugar Bowl are all so memorable exactly because of their rarity.

#2 – Experience Matters

With a month or more between the regular season finale and a bowl game, a month that includes individual awards shows and semester finals, many things can go wrong for a team. Coaches that have successfully prepared their teams in the past to perform strongly in the face of these challenges are more likely to be successful again. Obviously, each team, coach and season is different and overwhelming a poor opponent in one season does not mean a coach is some sort of genius. But in contrast to what all those mutual fund commercials tell us, when it comes to bowl games, past success can be an indicator of future success.

#3 – Offenses are High Maintenance

Like a super model or expensive sports car, offenses require constant maintenance. Today's offenses are based on rhythm and timing, concepts that can't be ignored for a few weeks without some lingering effects. Defense, however, is about aggression and following direction. It is about discipline. Discipline is, almost by definition, not lost in a few weeks of distractions. In bowl games, defenses can have an inherent advantage in a match-up of two relatively equal teams. I say 'can' not 'will' because it isn't a guarantee, but it seems to me, that you should always lean toward the team with a stronger defense as well as look to bet the Under.

Are these three factors a way of guaranteeing wins betting on bowl games? Of course not. There are no guarantees. But these three factors do seem to maximize the chance of winning – I certainly felt the pain when I ignored them.

Bowl Season

UCLA (-1) vs Baylor

There is really only one guarantee about this game: points. Both teams can move the ball and score. The difference is that UCLA can also occasionally stop the other team. Both of these teams play in conferences home to wide open spread offenses but UCLA has seen more success in at least slowing those high scoring offenses. They are also getting better each week with first year coach Jim Mora Jr.

Wins over Washington State, Arizona and Arizona State, have shown UCLA has found a way to win over spread offenses.

Baylor has really only played defense in one game this year, their massive upset of Kansas State. But that involved essentially stopping one player. UCLA has multiple threats in quarterback Brett Hundley and running back Johnathan Franklin. Just ask West Virginia and their 70-point scoring binge how Baylor handles a multi-headed threat.

Given a month to prepare, Mora can find a way to slow the Bears' offense. Last year, Baylor gave up 56 points to Washington in the Alamo Bowl – more points than Washington scored in any game all season.

Las Vegas on the morning of January 2nd looks like pretty much every other morning in the desert. Bright sun pours through my window. Cars trickle along Tropicana Avenue. Planes constantly deposit vacationers coming to town to win the fortune of a lifetime while other planes depart full of disappointed, exhausted partiers looking forward to going home just to get some rest.

It is a new month, a new year and very nearly the end of the football season, but the machinery that is Vegas just keeps humming along like a Japanese auto plant.

After a week away in the snowy mountains of Colorado pretending I belong with the 1% that awoke this morning with a larger tax bill due Uncle Sam, I returned to Las Vegas late last week. While others on my flight geared up for their "epic" Vegas New Year's Eve, I returned to work. In Colorado, I barely wrote and did no handicapping. I had laid bets to cheer on before I left and met up with an actual professional handicapper for a couple beers to understand how he does what he does but little new work was accomplished. I am not sure if I truly deserved a holiday vacation after spending the last four months chasing a dream, but I took one anyway.

The government can take my money and my guns but they can't take my vacations.

In truth, even upon return I struggled to return to 'work.' My handicapping of games last weekend was next to nothing – but given it was week #17, I figured quantitative analysis was moot anyway.

It is fitting that the NFL's week #17 comes amidst bowl season because they both present the same challenge in handicapping – a team's performance is driven more by the intangible than by any quantifiable factor. Is a college team motivated to play in a bowl game when they thought they deserved better? If an NFL team isn't playing for a spot in the post-season and are sixty minutes away from a much desired vacation, will they play hard?

Clearly, from my betting results, I am in no position to answer these questions. I lost more bets than I won, but through some smart money management (and luck, always luck), I sit here only slightly lower than I was when I left behind the glittering lights of the Strip back on December 20th.

Strangely enough, the bets I had been losing all season are the same ones that have rescued me, while the old stalwarts I could count on for a nice juicing of my bottom line have failed to come through. I won't make some clichéd joke about the Mayans or a Kim/Kanye spawn shifting the world's axis and changing my betting success, but maybe what worked early in the season is no longer applicable.

Over/Unders have been a scourge for me all season. Outside of a couple rare occasions, all season I seemed to find a way to be on the wrong side of these bets. If you need your team to score a bunch of points, there was no better way to ensure that happens than have me take the Under. But, strangely, in the bowl season that has changed. Call it the accumulation of a few weeks off, unfamiliarity with new foes, indifference at playing in bowls or jitters on a big stage for some of these teams, but betting Unders has been my most profitable strategy this bowl season and it started with BYU and San Diego State in the Poinsettia Bowl, where I bet the Under at 49 points. Remember that BYU beat Utah State 6-3, a Utah State team that averaged 34.9 points per season. I actually went out to eat dinner before halftime of this game and never seriously worried I would lose this bet. For the record BYU won 23-6, but whatever…Yeay, Cougars.

But just as some things changed, some remained the same – including my being wrong about a Big Twelve team's defense. In the days leading up to the Holiday Bowl, well after I had laid a bet on UCLA at +1, the line climbed up to around UCLA -2.5, so I was feeling pretty good betting early and being on the side of the money. Clearly I wasn't alone in thinking UCLA would handle Baylor. Which I guess is some sort of consolation – it means I am not the only idiot out there. UCLA got absolutely pounded by a Baylor team that had shown a defense exactly once all season, losing 49-26.

Looking for a spin on this game in hindsight, I would argue that Art Briles is a smart enough coach to have adjusted his bowl planning from last year's 67-56 scoring buffet against Washington, while Jim Mora, Jr. has never coached in college and has therefore never planned out a bowl preparation schedule. That is the logical answer. The emotional answer is that UCLA beat USC and almost won the Pac-12 and after that just couldn't be bothered to care at all about this game. L.A. types always look down on those from the heartland.

Speaking of teams from L.A., failing to get his team motivated for a bowl game in Texas, the only person that appeared less interested in being in El Paso on New Year's Eve for the Sun Bowl than USC coach, Lane Kiffin, was CBS announcer, Gary Danielson, whose brain chip malfunctions any time he can't spend three hours fluffing the SEC during a football telecast. I actually won several bets on Lane's lack of interest – with a bet on the Under (63) alone as well as parlaying the Under with Georgia Tech (+8). These lines seemed to assume the same high powered Trojan offense and toothless Tech defense would come to El Paso. USC playing without Matt Barkley in a windy stadium and against an opponent, I am pretty sure, they only scouted by watching their fictitious game in the movie *The Program*, had no offense. Tech's defense has secretly improved at least a little after firing defensive coordinator, Al Groh.

The Under was never in doubt and neither was a GT line where they could even lose by a touchdown and still cash. Winning the game by two touchdowns works just fine too. Just know that watching this awful game has ensured that Danielson will never give credit to a good team from the Pac-12 or ACC so in essence we were all losers.

After winning three of my four bets on New Year's Eve bowl games, I ended up only winning one of four on New Year's Day itself. However I was still up across the two days, thanks to betting more heavily on games on which I felt confident and keeping bets low on others. The Sun Bowl and the Chick-Fil-A Bowls saw big bets. The New Year's Day games saw smaller bets because I just didn't have a good feeling on most of the games. I bet on South Carolina (-4.5) because I hadn't been impressed by Michigan much this year and The Ol' Ball Coach has built a solid and balanced team in South Carolina that was one-turnover-fueled-implosion in Gainesville from being in the national title conversation.

Despite Jadeveon Clowney almost killing a man, this game remained close throughout. Thankfully, a lunch time engagement (with a man once featured a character on the Simpsons (!!!)) kept me from watching the second half of the game until immediately after South Carolina scored a touchdown with eleven seconds remaining to win by five. While I know it was entertaining, I am fine missing out on the stress of having my bet hanging in the balance the entire game.

After taking a week off from handicapping, the Outback Bowl was an interesting lesson in gambling 101. Had I bet early I would have gotten S. Carolina at -6 and lost my bet. I waited, bought at the bottom of the market and won (Note: the same thing occurred in the Rose Bowl with Stanford opening as a 6.5 favorite, closing as a 4-point favorite and winning by six). I wish I could claim some great strategy fueled this win, but it was just the lack of focus on this game until just before New Year's. And luck.

But, opening a new year with a win driven by buying at the right number was a good way to re-focus after a holiday week. Better than learning the lesson by being on the wrong side.

BCS Title game: Notre Dame (+10) vs Alabama
I love Notre Dame as a big underdog against Alabama in the BCS title game. I have bets on them at +9 and +10 already, totaling more money than any game I have bet to date. If it gets to +10.5 before kick-off I will lay more.

Unlike my middling NFL picks, though, this isn't based on the any other mathematical system, it is based on history.

Think back on the BCS title games when one team comes in as a prohibitive underdog – a team that hasn't looked impressive or played a great schedule. That team seems to always play it very close if not win outright. To me, the 2012 Notre Dame is a perfect reflection of the 2002 Ohio State Buckeyes team. They have played and won several very close games over unimpressive foes. They rely on defense and the offense not making mistakes. And in the national title game they play a fast, Southern team that is seriously looking at the word dynasty if they win again (Ohio State played defending national champion Miami). Ohio State won outright in double overtime (thanks to some dubious officiating) but regardless, they easily covered the two touchdown spread. I think Notre Dame does the same.

All of these beliefs that I have clung to for weeks have only been bolstered by the less than impressive showing by the SEC in the last week. LSU losing to Clemson (ACC pride!); Florida getting crushed by Louisville (Soon-to-be-ACC Pride!); Mississippi State losing to Northwestern; South Carolina squeaking by Michigan. Maybe, just maybe the SEC isn't as strong as people think when they see those jerseys. Maybe Bama has feasted on bad offenses and mediocre opponents (remember they didn't play South Carolina or Florida, two of the three best teams in the East).

Maybe Notre Dame has heard for a month how they don't deserve to be on the same field as the mighty SEC.

Maybe, just because Notre Dame is located in the Rust Belt people forget that they already beat USC and Oklahoma, teams with just as much speed as any SEC team.

For the first time since about 1988 I will relish my family's heritage and be a huge fan of the Irish. Fight on Notre Dame, fight on.

Coming into this little experiment, I expected to learn things; heading home from this with a new perspective and knowledge--understanding better how Las Vegas works and how professional bettors go about their business.

But there was one thing I never considered. The longer I have been here, the more money I have bet, the more money won, the more money lost, I have realized that it turns out that - for me - gambling isn't about the money.

A few weeks ago, I met a professional handicapper who admitted that he actually doesn't bet a lot on his own. His entire career involves handicapping games and selling his picks yet he personally doesn't bet a lot on a consistent basis. One could say that doesn't make sense – the 'put your money, where your mouth is' line of thinking. I (and he) argue, by putting his entire livelihood in the hands of those picks, there is no need to spend more money on those bets –his entire income is his bankroll. If he loses his picks consistently he does more than lose a bet, he loses reputation, customers and ultimately income.

While I do still bet regularly – that is kind of the point of what I am doing – I have found my bankroll has slowly come to be beside the point. My bankroll is down on the season, but I have dipped into less than 20% of my bankroll and there are only seven NFL games remaining on the season. Unless one or more of these remaining games shows a remarkable amount of value, I won't bet enough over the next three weeks to lose the rest of my bankroll or even lock in a profit on the season. Like a projected path for a hurricane, as the season has progressed, my ending bankroll is slowly tracking onto a path that leaves me with some but not out-sized losses.

So, at this point, it isn't about the money. It is about being correct. To think you not only know more than sports books but that people actually want to read your rambling thoughts, you have to possess a pretty healthy ego. I certainly meet that criteria, so as losses pile up, it is increasingly about the dent put in my ego more than the dent put in my bankroll that drives me nuts. I just hate that I missed something, that I misunderstood what was going to happen.

Sure, even the best gamblers can only expect to win 55 to 60% of their bets on a consistent basis but that doesn't help the bruising after a painful loss. The pain is especially acute on the games where I bet higher amounts, because those correlate to the game where I was even more confident. It is one thing to lose a game where I bet a small amount on something that appears unlikely. It is another to be confident in how something will play out and end up being completely and totally wrong.

Which brings us to Notre Dame.

My rationale for betting heavily on the Irish was based mostly on the historical patterns we have seen in BCS title games of big underdogs playing close and even winning outright.

The story of this game has been diagnosed repeatedly to this point so there is no reason to re-hash how out-manned Notre Dame ended up being--dominated on the offensive and defensive lines, a secondary not athletic enough to have a prayer of covering the Tide. The real question is what this does to Notre Dame's reputation long term. After getting crushed in their last two BCS Bowl games by SEC teams, can we ever believe in Notre Dame again?

If, in a year in which they beat USC and Oklahoma, they still aren't the athletic equal to an SEC team, will they ever be? If some future Irish team really is competitive with the best teams in the country will they be essentially blackballed – victims to the abysmal failure of January 2013? Can we ever believe in them? Yes, Notre Dame surprised us all by going undefeated this season, but did they actually do more harm to the long term prospects of the Irish as national champion contender by being given a chance this year?

As I sat at my seat in the Hard Rock casino, after about five minutes of game time I realized I was completely and totally wrong in looking at historical scenarios because I picked the wrong historical comparisons. Nick Saban has a semi-pro team and across four separate national title game appearances has honed his approach to preparation into a razor sharp blade. For the remainder of the game, I spent as much time scrolling Cantor's in-game betting menu looking for opportunities to make some money back as I did watching the Irish get slaughtered.

Under-manned, less talented teams can sneak up on over-confident, complacent teams. They can't sneak up on a Nick Saban team with a month to prepare.

So I lost a good sized chunk of money on the Irish. The lost money hurt but at the same time, thanks to the line never getting over +10.5, my losses were actually somewhat contained and my misery was more driven by being so utterly incorrect in my projection.

After having a fairly successful college gambling season, it sucks to go out on such a sour note. But that is the way of the Las Vegas. Now I have seven games left in the NFL to end on a higher note.

Another lesson that I have learned here: there is no brooding about losses in Las Vegas. To have any chance at success you have to forget wins and losses and always focus on the next game, confident that this time you will be correct.

A lesson that even Nick Saban could appreciate.

Line Movements

On New Year's Day, I pulled myself away from watching a series of losing Bowl game bets to meet a legendary bookmaker for lunch and an interview. The pretense of the interview was around prop bets and Vegas of old but Jimmy Vacarro has been working in casinos since the year I was born. To say he has seen a few changes here is about as big an understatement as saying Michael Jordan preferred winning to losing so I really just wanted to soak in a sliver of his knowledge.

After we discussed most of the main subjects I wanted to cover, we continued to talk while he finished his Chef's Salad and I polished off the last of my French dip sandwich (so much for eating healthier in the New Year). I explained this project and what I was doing in town. He asked what I thought; what had I learned about sports betting?

Not prepared to go from interviewer to interviewee, I thought for a moment, admitted I had learned a ton but that the more I learn, I realized that there was always more to learn. In a moment of utter desperation to put my thoughts into words (there is a reason I write; I need time to shape coherent thoughts), I fell back on a hackneyed cliché that felt somewhat appropriate sitting in a small deli.

I compared the sports betting world to an onion; where there seems to be never-ending layers of knowledge to navigate (yes, I can see you rolling your eyes).

To his credit, he didn't roll his eyes and groan (you could learn a lot from him) but instead nodded and admitted that even now he still learns something new nearly every day.

This chapter sort of represents reaching the second layer of the onion for me. It was something I struggled against the entire season. It is something that, for the most part, is not a big concern for a weekend bettor in Las Vegas for a couple days yet can end up having an enormous impact on winning or losing bets over the long term. Of course, it also requires more flexibility than many casual bettors have.

It is understanding which direction a point spread is moving and betting at the right time.

By nature I am apparently awful at guessing which way a line will move. All season, if I rushed to bet a line it would move in the opposite direction of what I feared: if I bet on a favorite, it would immediately drop to be a smaller favorite. If I bet an underdog, the line would immediately move to make them a bigger underdog. Once a line moves against a bet that has already been laid a bettor has two options – either add more to the bet so that at least he wins something if the final score ends up between where the initial bet was laid and where the subsequent bet was laid or let the initial bet ride and hope it doesn't come back to bite you. Basically, the question is: do you want more money at risk than you originally planned or do you leave value on the table?

I tried approach number one several times throughout the season; specifically I recall a bet on Western Kentucky back in Week #6. As usual, I laid a number of bets early in the week including putting money on WKU as three point favorites at Troy. Over the course of the week, WKU dropped all the way to be only a 1.5 point favorite and I added to my initial bet. Late in the fourth quarter the Hilltoppers led by two. One bet was a winner and one was a loser. Thankfully, the

Hilltoppers drove inside Troy's ten yard line and kicked a field goal with a minute remaining to win by five and I won both bets.

This WKU bet was just one example in which the middle created by a moving line could have cost me money, but it never did. By the time of the NFL playoffs, even though I still failed to predict which way the line would go I had yet to get burned by either adding to a moving line or letting a single bet ride.

And then the NFC Championship game happened. As you will see below.

In the wake of the NFC Championship game, I decided it was time to seek help from the experts. Sort of like my golf swing, I had been committed to figuring out everything on my own but finally realized I would never consistently succeed without at least a little professional help.

Dave Tuley is a long-time gambling journalist who I had met as part of my research on the LVH SuperContest. When he isn't document-ing all of the comings and goings in any corner of gaming, he also dabbles at sports betting – specifically betting on underdogs.

Following Dave on Twitter, I had been repeatedly impressed by his seeming perfect understanding of when to bet on a team. From the glances in the window I got on Twitter, Dave appeared to have figured out exactly how and when to bet to optimize his chances at winning.

In the week after the NFC title game I reached out to Dave to see if we could catch up and I could cast in his never-ending stream of knowledge.

It was because of this request that I found myself in a ballroom at the Treasure Island casino surrounded by hundreds of the best horse-racing handicappers in the world on an uncharacteristically cool, wet Saturday morning during the quiet weekend between the conference championships and the Super Bowl.

As part of his wide-ranging reporting on all things gambling, Dave was covering the national handicapping championships for the Daily Racing Form – the annual culmination of year-long local horse-racing handicapping contests across the country not dissimilar from the World Series of Poker.

While we watched races beaming in live from around the country and the tables of participants studied spreadsheets and videos on their laptops, I explained to Dave the help I wanted. Apparently, treating him as a great and wise oracle as I humbly replayed my painful loss the previous weekend appealed to Dave's charitable side. Seeking the one truth, like a traveler climbing the Himalayas, I hoped to find the secret to his success. However, the ultimate answer, as with most things in life, wasn't as simple or clear-cut as I had hoped. There was no little blue pill that illuminated the code of this Matrix.

Dave's approach starts with a heuristic and then requires a level of analysis. Depending on your level of time and commitment, you can choose how much effort you put in to getting the best line. Returning to my onion metaphor, it comes down to how many layers you want to peel. If you are a casual bettor only placing small recreational bets on a regular basis the heuristic may be enough. If you want to become a wiseguy – making a life through gambling - then a commitment is required--both of time and money.

First, the heuristic – a concept to simplify the timing of your bets:

Money comes in on favorites early in the week, and underdogs late in the week.

I guess I can come up with a level of logic that supports this: early money focuses on the favorites as the previous week's performance is still fresh in the mind. If you just watched Team A dominate and Team B struggle, that point spread may not be much of a deterrent, no matter the number. This obviously leads to the favorite line remaining steady or climbing as that money comes in but at some point an inflection point is reached – or a buy back happens in the parlance of gamblers. The favorite has become too big of a favorite, or even if it didn't climb, that recent performance starts to fade in the memory and that spread starts to look bigger. Money comes in late on the underdog.

To summarize: if you are betting a favorite, bet early before the line climbs or wait as long as possible as the buy-back continues to occur. If looking to bet the underdog, it is best to wait because the spread is likely to rise and you can get the underdog at a higher spread than where it opened. But don't wait too long or you miss the peak and get it coming back down.

Favorite, early; underdog late is easy enough. But how can you call the top of the market? Well, that is where the commitment is required.

There are two pieces of data critical to gauge which direction a line is moving – the percentage of bets coming in on each side and the detailed leans within a point spread.

To the latter first. Before a sportsbook moves a point spread by .5 or one point, it typically shades the Vig. Where Vigs typically start at -110 on both sides of a bet (bet $110 to win $100, with the $10"vig" being profit for the casino), if money starts to come in one side, the casino can move that side to -120 ($120 to win $100) and the other to +100. If one team is getting a disproportionate number of bets, the casino wants to make the bettor pay for it by reducing the payout on a win. This is an early warning sign that a point spread move is on its way. If a -120 doesn't stop the bets, then the point spread will start moving.

Similarly, the same information can be seen by looking at the percentage of bets coming in on one side versus the other. While, typically a bettor can't see the size of the bets being placed, he can see where the higher number of bets is coming.

Unfortunately, this information isn't generally available at one's fingertips, so beyond the time investment necessary to monitor the spreads regularly, a dollar commitment might be necessary. While spreads can be found online at web sites like pregame.com and donbest.com, there is often a delay in updates and only a portion of casinos are included. Pregame also utilizes a service called Sportsbook Spy where it shows the percentage of bets on each side of a match-up but again the speed at which this information is updated isn't clear.

For a serious bettor, this information is the equivalent of trying to use Yahoo's general stock market information to be a day trader. Information is advantage. To give the professional a necessary edge, services are available for an annual fee that provide detailed information on current point spreads at each casino including the current Vigs. These services post information in real time and also display the aggregate percentage of bets on each side across all the casinos.

For a bettor in Las Vegas looking to optimize their bets, these services are invaluable. Not only can you see how each spread is trending to pinpoint when to bet but you also get a snapshot of all the available casinos – ensuring you lay your bet at the best sportsbook. The trending of a spread is only half the battle, it is also critical to shop for the best spread. Sports books don't always move in lock step, spreads move in line with the action the casino is seeing. Casinos will often see a different profile of bets. This can be especially obvious when sportsbooks catering to public, vacationing bettors are compared to those with a higher percentage of local, sharp bettors, given how frequently the public and the pros see value differently.

These services aren't cheap but in the end if you are betting enough, one win from laying the bet at the right place and time may pay for the cost by itself. At Don Best, there are two pay service options. The first, without real-time spread updates costs over $1,000 per year. The professional version, with real-time point spread moves - the one "the pros use" - costs north of $5,000/year. Obviously, these aren't targeted to people that visit Las Vegas a few times a year and bet a few hundred per trip. It is a steep commitment but, if you are betting thousands per game all year long, it is a bargain. For most pros, its annual cost is less than the winnings of a single game.

Conference Championship Weekend

It is amazing that the week of the Conference championship games, with only three NFL games remaining until September, dawns and yet the NFL is only the 3rd biggest story in sports.

Somewhere deep underground in his lair on an unpopulated Japanese island, Roger Goodell is plotting a way to get back to the top of the sports section. I assume by the end of the week, he will suspend Adrian Peterson for being inhuman, Peyton Manning for being part cyborg or announce a new '2nd season' where each team will play five spring games. With no pads.

This should be the NFL's greatest month of the year and they are an afterthought thanks to a cyclist and the non-existent girlfriend of a college linebacker. I am kind of surprised Goodell hasn't already announced suspensions for both Lance Armstrong and Manti Te'o, just to see his name in print.

Thankfully, I got my game handicapping out of the way early this week to ensure I could get bets down at their optimal level (and then watched the lines move against me the moment I placed my bets, as usual). Since the Manti Te'o fake girlfriend story broke, my productivity levels have been approaching Paris Hilton levels. I can't look away from Twitter while I await the next nonsensical fact to drop. This story is sort of like modern art, I have no idea what I am seeing most of the time, yet I can't turn away from the shark carcass suspended in formaldehyde.

I refuse to speculate (publicly) on what the hell happened because nothing makes sense and no one -- possibly extending all the way to T'eo himself –knows what is going on.

That, of course, won't stop much of the media from jumping to whatever conclusion they feel pre-disposed to. Creating knee-jerk 'narratives' with too little information is the foundation of most large format journalism these days anyway. Narratives like, for example, a cancer survivor overcoming the odds and beating a cast of foreigners. Or a linebacker playing inspired by the struggles of a recently departed girlfriend.

As for Lance, call me cynical but when a guy beats cancer and then repeatedly wins a race filled entirely with people that are doping, I kind of assume he is doping as well; understanding relationships like this is why I did well on the ACTs. To say his 'confession' is old news is an insult to old news.

On the other side of this strange, weird week are the AFC and NFC Championships. A pang of pain shoots through me every time I see the Ravens in the title game knowing that should be the Broncos. But that won't stop me from betting. In fact, given there are only two games remaining and one involves two of my least favorite teams, let's go all in on gambling, picking both games against the spread and against the over/under line.

If it wasn't for gambling I would have a hard time stomaching the looming 3-hour Ray Lewis canonization that would make an awards show 'In Memoriam' look evenhanded and objective.

Sure, he once was involved in a man's death but as we learn over and over again, real life facts matter little compared to what the media has decided is the overarching story of someone. The media, having learned absolutely nothing this week, will once again hold up an athlete as all that is right with the world.

So cheers, Ray, in the media's eyes you will always be a great man and a great leader. Not like those charlatans, Lance and the girlfriend no one bothered to research.

<Quietly nudges body of knifing victim under the bed with toe of shoe>

SAN FRANCISCO AT ATLANTA OVER (48.5)

The system that I have been using projects a total of nearly 57, so who am I to argue? The offenses that have moved on the Forty-Niner defense this year have required receivers on the outside as well as a tight end threat (see: Patriots). Enter Tony Gonzalez who has finally won a playoff game to burnish his 'greatest tight end in history' re-sume (though Shannon Sharpe can't hear him over the shine coming off his three Super Bowl rings). The second half of last week's game showed that the Falcons' defense is incapable of tackling a mobile quarterback, especially when trying to stop a power running game. I think both teams can score a little and will blast through this line.

ATLANTA (+4) vs SAN FRANCISCO

Yes, we were all impressed by Colin Kaepernick's dismantling of the Packers last week but the dirty secret is that he just hasn't been that great on the road. Outside of at New Orleans and one great half at New England (neither of whose defenses will be confused with the '85

Bears), when he ventures from the friendly confines of Candlestick, Colin has looked like the inexperienced player he is. That horrid game at St. Louis. The implosion at Seattle. When he has faced solid defenses on the road, Kaepernick has not been the game changer he has been at home or against bad defenses. I am leaning to the Falcons because, I think this game is going to be close and I will happily bet on the home team with the best record in the NFC to lose by a field goal or less.

Full disclosure: Personally, I want the Forty-Niners to win. But separating heart from mind, being favored on the road by anything over a field goal seems like too much.

BALTIMORE AT NEW ENGLAND UNDER (51.5)

Again my system projects a different score than the line offered by Vegas. This time it suggests a score around 47. A look back at the history between these teams and it is easy to understand why. Outside of their week #3 game this year, these teams haven't scored more than 48 points in this match-up since 2007 (five match-ups). I just don't see a back and forth scoring fest like we saw in both AFC games last week. These teams know each other well; they know the other team's strengths and weaknesses. Last year's AFC title game between the same teams (two teams that have seen little turnover in personnel), totaled 43 points. Throw in a forecast of a cool windy day in Foxborough causing havoc with the passing game and I am riding with boredom this week.

BALTIMORE (+8) AT NEW ENGLAND

Ok, I refuse to always be a slave to the machine. This time, I am going against what the system projects. My numbers say New England is about 10 points better than Baltimore but I don't buy it, the system said the Broncos were 12 points better than Baltimore too. Baltimore may be this year's Giants; a team that is playing their best in the post season rendering projections based on their regular season performance irrelevant. Their defense is getting strong (and healthy) at the right time and Joe Flacco isn't making mistakes. I think the Ravens keep it close – as stated above they know how to play against the Patriots and are coming in riding a wave of confidence from that ridiculous win in Denver last week. A game they had no right to win.

But as I am sure we will be reminded repeatedly, the great and glorious leader, Ray Lewis, willed his overmatched Ravens to the win.

On the eve of a move to Las Vegas, when you tell others your plans, you always get the same reaction, "Oh man, I could never live there for that long." Taking the three-day benders that encompass most visits to town and extrapolating that experience out to six months and it is easy to see why that is the case; outside of a Kardashian or a Hilton, who could live like that for months on end?

Of course, the vast majority of my time here has been nothing like that. Sure, on the other side of my window the lights of the MGM shine to one side, the Hard Rock to the other and McCarran airport in between but that doesn't mean I spend all day, every day living the VEGAS life. For the most part, I treat it like just another place to live. I shop for groceries. I watch bad TV shows in my condo on weekday nights. I work out. In short, I act just like you do at home, though I think we can both agree maybe an extra trip to the gym wouldn't hurt. I have spent a good chunk of my adult life living out of hotels for months at a time in strange cities for consulting engagements, so maybe I have a unique perspective on this; but it was surprising how easy it was to transition to living in Vegas.

But that doesn't mean that there aren't still moments when I realize that, while it is home for me, it is still Vegas. And strange things happen in Vegas.

Such was my introduction to Championship weekend, when I sat around with a drug dealer and dispensed gambling advice to an out-of-town visitor.

On Friday night I had no plans so I ended up in the MGM sportsbook watching NBA and looking at the latest prop bets for the conference championship games. A small but talkative group of men were spread along the back wall discussing the NBA games and the coming NFL games. I joined in the discussions and as people departed I ended up alone talking with one other guy about the games and what we expected.

As part of our conversation, he mentioned he was visiting the MGM because he deals drugs – "just a little bit of blow, you know" - and has some clients in town visiting and staying at the MGM. I guess it is a compliment he entrusted me with this knowledge. Either that or he mistook my head cold as the mark of a possible client.

Before I could learn more about his enterprises, a man who had sat down near us, interrupted and asked for some help in reading the betting boards. My new friend - let's call him Avon after the greatest show on television I never watched - and I explained to the newbie what he was looking at and then we offered our suggestions on what to bet.

Staying true to my system, I offered up the Over on the Falcons/Niners game while Avon suggested he bet on the Ravens money line. After some more discussion, our innocent friend walked up to the window and placed two bets, $100 each on the San Francisco/Atlanta Over and Ravens money line.

So, yeah, that guy had a good Sunday. Maybe he even called Avon to help him celebrate.

And maybe my real future is in giving advice rather than betting, because he also had a better day than I did.

It is a weird quirk of nature that five victories can pale in the face of a single defeat.

It is called loss aversion: the concept that we fear a loss greater than we relish a victory. We mourn $100 lost much more than we celebrate $100 won. Based purely on economics it is an irrational, human emotion with little explanation--$100 is $100 is $100. Pac-Man Jones can make them all rain the same.

Yet I can't sit here and pretend to be above this feeling, for I am wallowing in it. I had a lucrative day, thanks to a couple excellent forecasts and astute in-game bets. I ended the day with more money than I started the day.

But it was one loss that continues to stab me in the ribs this morning like Ray Lewis outside a night club.

My very Vegas weekend continued even before the games on Sunday. I watched the games at the Hard Rock, which in addition to providing opportunities to make in-game wagers to add to or hedge my already laid bets, also gave the added entertainment of being in the immediate aftermath of hosting the AVN (that's Adult Video News) Expo the day before, which I now think of as the Super Bowl of people watching.

My empathy for the speculation aimed at every remotely attractive woman that happened to be in town was balanced by the inevitable game of "Porn Star, Hooker or Tourist" that I mentally played as each walked by (sorry, ladies). Unfortunately for you, I have no good stories to share outside of a minor freak out when a woman eating lunch looked vaguely familiar and the realization hit me that there was a chance it was due to her career of appearing on Cinemax late at night.

If that poor woman was in fact a porn star, that might have been the final square I needed to fill in on my 'Vegas Experiences' Bingo card. To date, I have already checked off: 'Meet a Drug Dealer'; 'See a Young Foreign Guy with Inexplicably Large Amounts of Money' (vaguely eastern European guy looking to transfer $62,000 at a local Bank of America); 'See an Athlete Gamble Obscene Amounts of Money (wassup Brian Urlacher!) and 'See a Prostitute' (basically every time I leave my condo).

I may not be living the Vegas lifestyle but that doesn't mean I am immune to my surroundings.

But, I digress… back to betting.

On the Sunday evening that the Conference championship match-ups were set, I completed my rudimentary handicapping and projected that Atlanta should be even, if not slightly favored over the Forty-Niners. Instead they were 3.5 point underdogs. I rushed down to the MGM sports book and laid a bet at +3.5, convinced that if I realized Atlanta was being underrated, so would others. A home team that is an underdog by more than a field goal? It seemed clear to me that money would move on Atlanta and the Falcons would soon be underdogs by a field goal or less. As it turned out, money poured in on San Francisco and the line climbed to Atlanta +4.5 before receding to +4. I faced the choice of piling more money on my bet or hoping the middle didn't bite me. I chose poorly after the Niners won 28-24, a 4-point win. By buying early, I lost the bet. It would be my only loss on the day and yet the only bet I still even think about.

The fact that the loss on Atlanta bothers me so much is even stranger in that I hedged it successfully, offsetting some of that loss. In the first half when Atlanta took a 17-point lead, I laid a bet on San Francisco +9.5. It seemed clear to me that Atlanta wouldn't hold that big of a lead (see the previous week's sacrifice of a 20-point lead to the

Seahawks) so I put money on the Niners to buy into the coming rally and hedge my Atlanta bet. Unfortunately it was less than half of the original bet but at least I won back some of my Atlanta losses.

The pain of the Atlanta loss also makes little sense because my single biggest bet of the weekend was on the Over at 48.5. After a high scoring first half that saw 38 points put on the board, it looked likely that the Over would cash so when the Niners started the second half with a strong drive, the in-game betting at Cantor jumped to 62.5 and was paying even money (it would spike to 66.5 after the subsequent Niners' TD). I decided to put down money at Under 62.5 as a hedge to a complete stop in scoring with the hope that there would be just enough scoring to win both. Sure enough that initial Niner 2nd half touchdown combined with a touchdown in the final minutes, tipped over the original bet totaling 52 points. When the Falcons failed to respond, the 2nd bet hit as well. I finally hit the smooth creamy middle of winning two offsetting bets. Twinkies for everyone.

I won twice as much money on these bets as I lost on Atlanta and the points. Yet I haven't stopped thinking about Atlanta. Damn you, dirty birds.

Moving to the AFC championship game, I never got a good feel for the spread on this game. My system projected Pats by ten, but I leaned toward Baltimore. I wanted to bet Baltimore as Underdogs by more than ten or, alternatively, if the Pats could have gotten to be favored by seven or less before the game I probably would have bet on them. But with the line floating between eight and nine, I just stayed away.

Instead I did bet on the Under at 51.5, based on the close, long history between these two teams. They know each other too well to allow for a high scoring game on a cold, windy day. Sure enough, the game started very slowly. In the first half, the in-game dropped all the way to 40.5, so I laid some money assuming there would be at least some jump in scoring in the 2nd half. The Pats were already checked out by that point but the Ravens did just enough to push the total to 41, winning 28-13.

I should be thrilled with being so right about my projections. For the most part, both of the Conference Championship games followed the script I wrote of what I expected. Even better for the most part, I profited from those expectations, which has not always been the case this season.

Most remarkably, on multiple occasions I hedged pre-game bets with in-game bets in hopes of hitting the Twinkie and won those as well. I think that has worked successfully about three times all season, and I did it correctly twice in one day. As Ice-Cube once said, I have to say it was a good day.

Except for one mistake on my part that I just can't get over.

In recent years, social scientists have begun to debate whether loss aversion exists. On a Sunday in Las Vegas, I can 1,000% guarantee it does.

The Super Bowl & Prop Betting

(Adapted from an article that appeared on SBNation Longform in January 2013)

With 3:30 remaining in the third quarter of Super Bowl XX, the Chicago Bears led the New England Patriots 37-3. The Bears offense lined up on New England's one-yard line prepared to put the final sprinkles on their Super Bowl championship sundae. At the snap, William "Refrigerator" Perry, the Bear's rookie defensive lineman jumped from his stance in the Bears' backfield, took a hand-off from quarterback Jim McMahon and lumbered across the unnaturally green turf of the New Orleans Superdome. He split the defenders and, like an appliance tumbling from the back of a truck, fell into the bright red end zone, the final touchdown of the season for the fabled '85 Bears on their way to a 46-10 victory.

After the game, amidst the locker room celebration of one of the most dominant seasons the NFL had seen, the only cloud in sight hung above Walter Payton. Payton, the long-serving veteran of the Bears and one of the great running backs in league history, bristled at not scoring a touchdown in his only Super Bowl appearance. He believed coach Mike Ditka had been swept up in the hoopla over Perry, who during the season had generated Kardashian-esque amounts of hype as an over-sized and very part-time running back.

But Payton wasn't the only person disappointed by Perry's touchdown plunge. Fifteen hundred miles to the west in Las Vegas, the moment Perry theatrically spiked that ball, sportsbook managers up and down the Strip cringed and cursed.

In the buildup to the game, Las Vegas sportsbooks looking to capitalize on the country's fascination with the massive gap-toothed rookie had posted odds on whether Perry would score a touchdown. As Ditka publicly down-played Perry's role, the odds soared to as high as 75 to 1, potentially earning bettors $750 in winnings for every ten dollars bet on Perry to score. Then the national media picked up the story, relishing another colorful hook associated with a team that had created their own music video mid-season. As the publicity flowed in to Las Vegas, so did money. By kick-off the odds dropped to 2 to 1. Now a ten dollar bet on Perry would only earn back twenty bucks.

Still, the Perry touchdown won hundreds of thousands of dollars for bettors all along the Strip. For the casinos however, that loss would be spare change compared to the millions and millions of dollars they would ultimately make because of that one single play.

ﾉﾉﾉﾑ

Today, prop bets have become synonymous with the Super Bowl. Bets on who scores the first touchdown of the game, how many yards each quarterback throws for, whether a safety occurs or even if the opening coin toss results in "heads" or "tails" are commonplace today. It's all part of the now-common narrative that results from two weeks of hype leading to the biggest sporting event in America. Although prop bets and the Super Bowl seem made for one another, the story behind the prop bet doesn't start with the Super Bowl. It doesn't even start with football or in the desert of southern Nevada.

ﭏﭏﭏﭏ

In the early 20th century, Las Vegas was a small desert outpost still decades away from becoming the center of gambling in America. Back then, someone wanting to bet on a sporting event didn't travel across the country; they went across town – or across the street. In no town was this more true than in Boston.

Gambling wasn't an underground activity in Boston; it was right out in the open, especially at Fenway Park, home of the Red Sox. Baseball and gambling had always been as closely related as siblings, but in Boston they were Siamese twins. The section of stands known as the right field pavilion that paralleled the foul line essentially belonged to gamblers. As the game went on their activities more resembled the pit of a stock market than fans at a game; men frantically waving dollars in the air and offering odds on anything and everything. They were so brazen that on June 16, 1917, hundreds rushed the field during the rainy 5th inning in hopes of forcing a postponement of the game before their losses tied to a 2-0 Red Sox deficit to the White Sox became official.

It was no coincidence that the greatest gambling scandal in American sporting history, the 1919 Black Sox scandal, began in Boston. At the Hotel Buckminster, only a block from Fenway, White Sox first baseman 'Chick' Gandil and Joseph "Sport" Sullivan, a notorious Boston gambler hatched the scheme in which some White Sox conspired to throw the 1919 World Series against the Cincinnati Reds. A gambling syndicate, of course, funded and also profited from the enterprise.

Into this atmosphere, in 1921, Julius Reizner was born in nearby Taunton, Massachusetts. Reizner, nicknamed Sonny due to his positive disposition, gambled before he even had money, betting on games of marbles as a young boy. By his teens he was spending his off-hours at pool halls and in the pavilion at Fenway Park, where even after the

Black Sox scandal the gamblers still held sway. As Reizner wrote in his book *The Best of Sonny Reizner:* "Propositions were thrown back and forth in the stands in those days on just about every pitch. There would be a price if the pitch would be a ball or a strike, a price if the batter would get a hit, or walk or make an out, a price on scoring a run, etc.," so called "do they or don't they" bets that rendered the outcome of the game almost entirely irrelevant.

Years later, Reizner told a reporter, "Now that I think about it, I guess that's [Fenway Park] where the idea for proposition wagering was born. When I was in a position to do so, it was only natural to extend it to the Super Bowl."

Reizner bounced around a series of jobs in greater Boston, working in a warehouse and helping run the family antique store with his mother, but his day jobs simply funded his true career as a bettor. He bet on anything and everything, from invented dice games to sports. He won a series of bets during the 1958 World Series, rolling over the winnings until losing a $100,000 bet on Game Seven when the Yankees dumped Milwaukee.

He was almost fifty when he came to Las Vegas in 1970. For the first time he moved behind the betting counter, joining a small race and sportsbook called Churchill Downs.

ノノノ⌐

Although Jimmy Vaccaro was born a generation after Reizner, he too was swept up by gambling, which flourished almost everywhere as the American economy experienced an unprecedented post-war boom. Vaccaro grew up in Western Pennsylvania, in the shadows of the plants and factories that fueled America's growth. Like Reizner, Vaccaro was a gambler by nature before it became his vocation. His brother, six years his senior, got him started and Vaccaro bet parlays before he reached puberty. He moved to Youngstown, Ohio to attend college in the 1960s but left without a degree seven years later. His real education came from time spent in Youngstown's pool halls, barrooms and back alleys, wherever men gathered after work to let off steam, play craps and bet on the ponies, a boxing match or the ballgame.

In 1975, without a real job and with only $140 in his pocket, Vaccaro moved to Las Vegas. A friend steered him to Michael Gaughan, who ran the Royal Inn. Gaughan helped Vaccaro enroll in a blackjack dealer's class that launched Vaccaro's career.

At the time, sports gambling was an afterthought in the burgeoning gambling scene in Las Vegas. With a 10% tax levied on sports bets, the larger casino/hotels believed the risk and the hassle outweighed the potential gain. They ignored sports betting, leaving it to the small specialist houses such as the Churchill Downs where Reizner worked. But in the early '70s, Nevada Senator Howard Cannon decided to juice the Nevada economy by making Vegas a sports betting destination. He helped spearhead legislation that ultimately reduced those taxes to 0.25%. The large casinos quickly became disenchanted, seeing their customers hopping into cabs to visit independent sportsbooks, and instead started building their own. The casinos needed someone to run them and they naturally looked to the men most familiar with sports betting – experienced bettors.

After working briefly at a few other sportsbooks, Reizner ended up at the Howard Hughes-owned Castaways casino, managing the Hole-in-the-Wall sportsbook. Michael Gaughan tapped Vaccaro to start the sportsbook at the Royal Inn. As Vaccaro describes it, "Michael Gaughan called me upstairs. He said, 'Do you know how to run a sportsbook?' And I said 'No.' You know what his answer was? 'Good, neither do I, we will start one together.' "

Historically, bets in sporting books had been limited to only three options: (1) Moneyline bets (a wager on which team will win a game at adjusted payouts for favorites and underdogs); (2) Point spread bets (where points are adjusted and the favorite and underdog pay the same amount); and (3) Totals bets (also known as Over/Under – i.e., how many total points will be scored). With their clientele limited to a small band of hardcore sports bettors, the independent sportsbooks had little incentive to expand betting offerings.

But the new generation of former gamblers now managing the large hotel sportsbooks started looking beyond the hardcore bettors to a new customer: casual vacation bettors. The hotels courted these inexperienced, recreational bettors by trying to stand out from the crowd. New, more inventive bets were one way to attract attention. Reizner, recalling the scene in the right field pavilion at Fenway Park, was one of the leaders of the movement. He offered lines on previously ignored sports like NASCAR, tennis and even the Boston Marathon. Jackie Vaughan at the El Cortez went even farther and took bets on where Skylab, a space station that had ended its useful life, would crash land upon its return to Earth. On that bet, Australia, a longshot at 30 to 1, came in.

The sportsbooks knew vacationers from places like Youngstown and elsewhere were looking as much for a story as profit. "Some of them made bets just to take the ticket home with them," Vaccaro remembers, "To show their other friends....this is the crazy stuff I was betting on."

At the same time, Caesar's Palace started hosting large Super Bowl parties to draw crowds, inviting ex-players and ex-coaches to mingle with the public. For the first time, Las Vegas saw an influx of bettors for the Super Bowl. All along the Strip sportsbooks started looking beyond the standard three bets to separate some of these visitors from their money. Still, by the end of the '70s most casinos offered just a handful of prop bets. Many were considered oddities, ignored and dismissed by both the sportsbooks and most bettors. No one would ever have confused Vegas of the 1970s with the right field pavilions of Fenway Park.

ﺟ ﺟ ﺟ

On March 21, 1980, nearly 25 million people tuned in to the season finale of the primetime soap opera *Dallas*. In the final scene, Ewing family scion J.R., played by actor Larry Hagman, was shot by an unknown assailant, leaving viewers hanging. The entire country spent the summer not just discussing the mystery, but even wearing T-shirts asking the question on everyone's mind: "Who Shot J.R.?"

Sonny Reizner saw an opening. He seized on the national phenomenon and put up odds on suspects, not just characters on the show, but real-life figures like Dallas Cowboys coach Tom Landry whose only connection to the program was the aerial shot of Cowboy Stadium used during the opening credits. The press flocked to the story and as bettors rushed to put their money down on an entirely fictional and ultimately absurd question Reizner gained national attention for the Hole-in-the-Wall sportsbook. As he later recalled in his book, "Most of the people were not your typical sports bettor. Little old ladies from Iowa wanted to bet. Baptist ministers wanted to bet. Rabbis wanted to bet. Thirteen-year old kids wanted to bet. Everybody thought they knew who shot J.R. and were willing to invest a few dollars on the outcome."

Ultimately, however, the Nevada Gaming Control Board stepped in. The Board took the bet seriously and rightly assumed that someone on the production staff of the show knew who shot J.R. and therefore had an unfair advantage. The Board forced Reizner to remove the lines and refund all bets.

No one in Las Vegas legally won any money by correctly betting on J.R.'s scheming mistress and sister-in-law, Kristin Shepard (played by Mary Crosby), but the board's decision had a lasting impact. Although Nevada casinos remain restricted from posting betting lines on non-sporting events today, they learned something even more valuable: the value of the publicity associated with setting a betting line on something that captures the public's imagination.

In the wake of the Who Shot J.R.? spectacle, all of the sportsbooks along the Strip started looking for a legal wager that would have a similar impact and become a part of the national conversation. While the Super Bowl and March Madness continued to grow as the biggest gambling events of the year, prop bets, for a time, still remained an afterthought.

Then came the Fridge and the bet on whether he would score a touchdown in Super Bowl XX. For the first time since "Who shot J.R.?" a wager intrigued an entire country, not just the bettors lining up at the sportsbook windows each week.

By then Vaccaro had moved to the MGM. He recalls getting a phone call from a Chicago Tribune writer, amazed that someone could bet on whether Perry would score. As Vaccaro recalls, "We got national publicity...this proposition went through the roof...everyone in the freaking world called us."

The MGM and Caesar's may have lost money on the Fridge but they had also gained the valuable insight that Super Bowl hype and the prop bet were a match made in a very profitable heaven.

The publicity didn't just benefit the casinos. The men who created them also profited, becoming the faces of the casinos where they worked. As the small, older casinos were replaced by the monoliths we see today, the big casinos wanted the biggest names to represent their sportsbooks. Guys like Sonny Reizner suddenly became larger than life. He moved from Castaways to the Frontier before opening the Rio in 1989.

Vaccaro himself later moved from the MGM to help open Steve Wynn's Mirage, where he created his most unique prop bet. In a 1995 special episode of the *The Simpsons* paying homage to Dallas, Vaccaro provided (fictional) odds on who had shot Mr. Burns in the cartoon's own season-ending cliffhanger. *(Maggie Simpson was the surprise culprit.)*

While men like Vaccaro and Reizner became national figures, the next generation of bookmakers looked to see just how far they could push betting options. After all, despite the losses on the Fridge bet, prop bets, due to their ability to attract new bettors and garner publicity, proved to be a wise investment.

❧❧❧

In the late 1980s, Jay Kornegay was new to Las Vegas, and just learning the ropes at the Imperial Palace sportsbook. Unlike the founding sports book bookmakers such as Vaccaro and Reizner, Kornegay hadn't spent his youth gambling in pool halls or the pavilion at Fenway. Nevertheless he had become intrigued by the industry on a senior year spring break trip and joined the profession after graduating from Colorado State.

Despite not growing up surrounded by gambling, Kornegay and others of his generation quickly embraced the notion of looking at games as more than just wins, losses and point spreads. Gather any group of sports fans together for very long in a gambling environment and inevitably challenges are leveled and wagers made – most extending far beyond the standard offerings of a sportsbook. Behind the desks at places like the Imperial Palace, conversations among the staff were never limited to who would win a game.

For example, when the 'Showtime' Lakers faced the 'Bad Boy' Pistons in the 1988 and 1989 NBA Finals the staff of the Imperial Palace – banned from betting at their own sportsbook – made private bets among themselves. How many games will be played in the series? How many points will Magic score? Who scores more – Magic or Isiah? Will Magic have more assists than Rodman has rebounds? Regulars overheard these informal bets and debates among staffers and soon asked to join in. To accommodate their interest the Imperial Palace soon posted these types of prop bets on all kinds of sporting events.

None, however, proved as popular as prop bets on the biggest betting event of the year, the Super Bowl. After the success of the Perry bet in 1986, Super Bowl prop bets rapidly grew in popularity. By the early 1990s most books offered somewhere between thirty and fifty prop bets for each Super Bowl. Then circumstances well outside of Las Vegas' control threatened to impact their business on the biggest sport betting day of the year.

Beginning in 1990, for six of the next eight years the Super Bowls were one-sided blow-outs as NFC powers annually dominated over-matched AFC opponents with scores of 55-10, 52-17, 49-26 and 35-21. Even worse, many of these games were *predictable* blow-outs, and predictable blow-outs generate little betting interest. In response, the casinos needed to provide bettors other incentives to gamble. Prop bets unrelated to the outcome but not resolved until the clock runs out were the obvious answer.

The casinos soon began manufacturing these bets as rapidly as Toyota produces cars, and most were soon offering a hundred or more options, including some that crossed the boundaries of individual sports. Michael Jordan was the most popular athlete in the world at the time, a magnet whose every move attracted attention. If there was little doubt or interest in wagering that the Cowboys would out-score the Bills, the sportsbooks figured there might be more suspense as to whether or not Dallas would out-score Jordan in his game that weekend. Bettors seized on such opportunities, throwing money at wagers that maintained interest in the game to the end.

Prop bets established a beachhead as an integral part of the Las Vegas Super Bowl experience. Even after the Super Bowls became competitive again in 1998 when Denver beat Green Bay in arguably one of the greatest Super Bowls ever played (at least for Broncos fans), the popularity of the prop bet never waned. As Vaccaro remembers today, "It just fed itself. It just kept getting bigger and bigger and bigger."

Sonny Reizner retired from the Rio in 1996, spending his last few years as an observer of the craze he helped to popularize. In 2002, he passed away at the age of 81, winning his own prop bet in life expectancy for a man of his generation. Vaccaro eventually left the Mirage and took over Lucky's, a chain of Nevada sportsbooks. Last year British betting giant William Hill bought Lucky's where Jimmy now plays a sort of 'Bookmaker Emeritus' role as Director of P.R.

In recent years, the prop bet craze that Reizner and Vaccaro helped foster has seen another bump in popularity due to the rise of the offshore sportsbooks. Not restricted by Nevada's rules regarding non-sports bets, offshore sportsbooks, although illegal in the U.S., offer a far broader selection of betting options than their domestic counterparts.

For the Super Bowl no option is left untouched, whether a bettor is a sport fan or not. For the musically inclined, bets on the duration of the Star Spangled Banner and the first song sung by Beyonce during this year's halftime performance are available.

Those more interested in fashion than football can also bet on whether Beyonce will be showing cleavage during that first song and whether the Harbaugh brothers will both wear hats. The current odds heavily favor both cleavage and hats.

Bets can even be placed on the bettors themselves – there are odds on the amount of money Nevada will pull in on Super Bowl bets - *Inception* meets Super Bowl prop betting.

The Nevada Gaming Control Board, apparently recognizing that their restrictions have put casinos at a disadvantage to these offshore sportsbooks, now offers casinos an opportunity to apply for an exemption to post non-sporting event lines. However, the bureaucratic requirements are daunting, and few bets seem to be worth the effort. Kornegay, however, looks at the American presidential election and sees a near endless possibility of innovative prop bets. He believes that betting on the Presidential election could eventually dwarf any sporting event, the Super Bowl included. Between those blindly betting on their preferred candidate and those hedging against the wrong candidate winning, it is easy to envision the massive interest in betting on an election. Even bets on items peripheral to the outcome of the election would likely generate interest – whether the duration of an acceptance speech, the time of the loser's concession, or the tie color chosen by the winner, Presidential election betting options seem endless. The right election prop bet could light the imaginations of every voter in the same way the Perry bet once captured NFL fans.

While the sportsbooks of Nevada may envy the freedom enjoyed by the offshore books, there is, as yet, little real concern about their competitive impact. No bet placed in front of a computer alone at home can compete with the camaraderie of sitting in a sportsbook surrounded by hundreds of other sports fans. The finances of Super Bowl betting for Nevada bear this out.

Where prop bets once accounted for maybe five percent of a sportsbooks' total Super Bowl action, prop bets can now represent as much as 40 to 50 percent. In 2012, a total of nearly $94 million was bet on the Super Bowl at Nevada sportsbooks. That means that $35 to $45 million was wagered on Super Bowl prop bets alone.

This year, in the days and weeks before the conference championship games, Kornegay, who is now the Vice President of Race and Sports Book Operations at the LVH, met with his staff to review what prop bets will be offered for this year's Super Bowl. To the south at William Hill U.S., Vaccaro and his compatriots did the same.

The starting point for this year's wagers is last years' offerings . The prop bets that didn't see much action or those that require too much effort relative to their response were removed. Potential new bets were brainstormed, the staff guessing which teams would emerge from the championship games (inevitably getting one wrong) and starting their work on updating the data for this year.

On the Thursday following the conference championship games, LVH released this year's Prop bet menu. Stretching to 25 pages and providing over 300 wagering options, it is Las Vegas' answer to War and Peace. Limited to on-field action, the LVH focuses heavily on individual players while also offering opportunities to bet on nearly every element of game action.

Alumni of Nevada, Delaware and all fans of quarterback play can bet on practically every decision made by Colin Kaepernick and Joe Flacco. Total passing or rushing yards, number of completions, number of touchdown passes, whether they complete their first pass, whether they throw an interception or touchdown first, their longest rush, their longest completion, and whether they throw a touchdown in each of the 1st, 2nd, 3rd or 4th quarters specifically are all available among many others.

The cross-sport bets have matured far beyond the offerings from Michael Jordan's prime. There are still opportunities to wager whether the Niners out-score Kobe or LeBron but there are also wagers on whether Lionel Messi scores more goals against Valencia than Frank Gore scores touchdowns; whether Sidney Crosby scores more goals against the Capitals than Kaepernick throws touchdowns and whether Lee Westwood's final round score at the Phoenix Open is lower than Ray Rice's total rushing yards.

Even people who would rather cheer for the referees than the teams playing can profit by wagering on total penalty yardage and which Harbaugh brother challenges a call first.

While the menu has broadened, so has the rigor in developing lines. The days of a line moving from 75 to 1 all the way to 2 to 1, as the prop bet over Williams Perry's touchdown did, are gone. Now, there is simply too much information too widely available; each bet creates more data that is in turn input for future bets. For the commonplace prop bets now posted annually, updating is so streamlined it requires little more than replacing the names of the Giants and Patriots with the Forty-Niners and Ravens. New prop bets, however, are heavily analyzed before ever being offered to the general public. There is still no room for error.

For the sportsbooks, the novelty is gone and today prop bets are as predictable as any other kind of wager. Many of the bets have been up for years and the sportsbooks understand how the betting public reacts. As Kornegay says, "People want to see things happen," so there is always a bias towards bets on the "Over" on an Over/Under bet, or the "Yes" on a Yes/No bet. Yet at the same time, this advantage is counterbalanced by the increased sophistication of the betting public. Greater acceptance of gambling coupled with the proliferation of gambling information available on the internet and on social media means that today a member of the general public potentially can pose as big of a risk to the casinos as the wisest wiseguy.

All of this means that the prop bets we see today, while more wide-ranging in their breadth, are also tougher to beat. Yet that does not mean they are infallible, particularly to a professional gambler.

Geoff Kulesa, a professional handicapper who runs the Wunderdog Sports handicapping service doesn't look at the prop bets as a distraction or diversion to keep himself entertained if the big game ends up being dull. He views them as opportunities for value.

"What's easier is finding bets that don't get a lot of attention," he writes in an email. "You can spot errors more often in these lines. You can find places where the oddsmakers make consistent mistakes that don't get fixed year after year. Bottom line: there's more value in the prop bets; they are easier to beat."

He has his own vast databases to mine for prop bet data, looking to see where the odds posted by the casinos differ from his own calculations. "I run stats to see how certain bets have performed in the past," he writes. "I then generally find a 'cut-off' point for a prop bet in which I feel comfortable betting it if the line/odds exceed some threshold for me."

Despite applying more discipline in their development, the sportsbooks still don't view prop bets as enormous moneymakers. Although profit is earned through the shrewd management of the vig (the commission taken by the casino) and by moving odds quickly in response to money coming in, with low bet limits even the most profitable individual prop bet pales in comparison to bets on the game result. Vaccaro estimates he will lose no more than ten thousand dollars on any single prop bet, while millions and millions can swing on whether or not the Forty-Niners beat the Ravens. It is an object lesson in diversification; even if the casinos see a big loss on one prop bet, that loss will likely be offset by wins on the majority of the other 299 available bets.

As it was back in 1986 with the Fridge, and with the question of "Who shot J.R.?", the real value in prop bets remains in the publicity they generate for the casinos. A prop bet that captures the imagination of the public, even if it loses for the casino, can generate outsized returns as it entices new bettors to come to the casino, open their wallets and hope for a story to take back home. Either way, the house always wins.

♪♪♪♪

On New Year's Day, I met Jimmy Vaccaro at Ellis Island, a small casino located off the Strip where Vaccaro's employer, William Hill US, runs the sportsbook. The casino feels different from the monstrosities that have popped up along the Strip in recent years, all bright lights, high ceilings and white marble. In contrast, Ellis Island's main casino floor is small enough to circumnavigate in 30 seconds, darkened by burgundy walls and crowded with red pleather chairs stationed before each slot machine.

The sportsbook is a tiny room located just steps from the whirling lights of the slots, wedged in next to a barbecue restaurant. There is no VIP section or sprawling soft couches. There are eighteen desks and chairs lined up in three rows of six that face a betting desk and a bank of TVs and betting boards spread across the wall.

Vaccaro, wearing a white sweatshirt and a couple day's stumble on his face, with thick white hair pulled straight back from his forehead waits at the counter.

Over a Chef Salad at the small café just across the casino floor, Jimmy talked about a Vegas long passed, casinos that are barely a memory and the characters that built this town who are now on the cusp of being forgotten. Sitting here in this small, old-fashioned casino it is easy to picture Las Vegas as it was in the '70s. The only things missing are bell bottoms, butterfly collars and a Bee-Gees song playing in the background.

Back in the sportsbook, some of the customers are using William Hill's in-game betting application on their smartphone to bet on events in real time. Customers can now bet on full game point spreads adjusted to reflect the current score or wager on the outcome of the current drive. In-game, real time betting is the next big wave in the ever-rising tide of prop betting opportunities.

It may require the latest in technology to do it, but we are on our way right back to the beginning –betting on every minute aspect of the game as it unfolds before our eyes.

The only thing bettors can't do here in the casino is rush the field if the game starts going against them.

The Super Bowl

SAN FRANCISCO (-3.5) VS BALTIMORE
As should be expected for the biggest gambling event of the year, there appears to be little value on bets for the Super Bowl. My system came up with the Niners by 6.5, so I waited as early Baltimore money came in this week and moved an opening Niners -5 line down to -3.5 before betting. I would really love to get the Niners to -3 or lower but I don't see that happening. If anything it is going back up.

The obvious comparison for this Ravens team is the Giants teams that won two Super Bowls in the last six years. A quarterback leading a limited offense by minimizing mistakes and making occasional big plays. A defense that looked questionable all season rising up in the playoffs to out-play their season-long performance. You could even make an easy comparison of Ray Lewis and Michael Strahan (older player in his final season, who gets by on reputation more than performance). With that logic, the Ravens are the obvious play. As much as I love historical parallels, in this game there seems to be one giant asterisk to this comparison. And I don't mean an asterisk in the 'Ray Lewis is doing this by taking PEDs' sense.

In both the playoffs and in the Super Bowl, those Giants teams defeated teams that relied on high scoring, pass-happy offenses and mediocre defenses that would do enough to let the offense out-score the other team. In both seasons the Giants beat both the Packers and Patriots – teams that follow this script year in and year out – by putting immense pressure on the quarterbacks while doing just enough on offense to win the game in thrilling fashion. The problem with applying this script to the Ravens is that, while their run to date has aligned, the Forty-Niners do not fit the script at all.

The Ravens can't just hit Colin Kaepernick in the face a couple times and watch him fold like Tom Brady. The Niners would rather hit you right back than throw it over you. The Falcons put pressure on Kaepernick in the NFC title game and San Francisco turned instead to a grinding running game and intermediate passing game utilizing Vernon Davis. Offensively the Niners don't look like the Packers or Patriots. If anything, they are migrating to an offense similar to the Redskins with a power running back and mobile quarterback. The Redskins put up 31 points on the Ravens. The Ravens scored 28 in that loss to Washington, but no one is confusing the Redskins defense with the Forty-Niner defense.

If we want to continue the comparison of Giants and Ravens, the next obvious point is that the Giants' went into San Francisco and won last year's NFC title. But they won in overtime, after getting two gift muffed punts. And don't forget last year's Niner offense with Alex

Smith and few quality wide receivers was nowhere near as dangerous as this year's rendition.

I think it will be close and low-scoring but the Forty-Niners hold on for a 27-20 win.

SAN FRANCISCO/BALTIMORE UNDER (48)

Some simple math from the last sentence and you can tell, I think this barely covers. The total opened around 50 on Sunday evening after the two conference championship games but was immediately bet down to around 48 before I laid this bet on the following Monday morning. Given two strong defenses and the usual jittery starts to Super Bowls it is easy to expect a low scoring game but with the Ravens big play potential and the efficiency of the Forty-Niners offense, I don't think this is a lock. I laid the bet so obviously I think Under is the better option of the two, but I retain little confidence.

LAMICHAEL JAMES – TOTAL RECEIVING YARDS OVER 8.5 YARDS (+140)

The rest of these bets are some props I found after wading through the novella of bets posted by the LVH. Given how much time I spent thinking about prop bets lately it seemed like I should bet a few. When I first saw this, I assumed the pay-out was wrong – how could James NOT get 8.5 yards receiving? But a quick review of his season shows why. Five receptions for 40 yards on the season. Not a coincidence that he averages 8 yards per catch is it? Maybe this is a sucker bet with a surprisingly low yardage number and high payout but I think it is value. James didn't catch his first pass until week #13. He caught one in each of the two playoff games. In short, he is being worked into the offense more each week. All he needs are one or two swing passes or screens to easily cover this. With his speed and the lack of speed in the Ravens linebacking corps (see: retiring linebacker who resorted to sucking deer antler spray this season), I would expect James sees more playing time than has been his average. It is a fine line between trap and lock. This one smells closer to lock to me.

FRANK GORE – SCORE A TOUCHDOWN IN THE FIRST HALF (+220)

The key to me for betting prop bets is to look for bets that show value and also align with your expectations for how the game will play out. Or, alternatively, show value and hedge other bets that align with your expectations for how the game will play out. These first two are based on my belief that the Niner offense will adapt and prosper against the Ravens' defense. James to run past the defense with his speed. Gore to run right at them. We know if the Niners get inside the five-yard line, Gore will get at least one or two shots at the end zone. Winning over two times my bet, it is worth it to bet he will find that end zone before half time.

HAIL MARY OF THE WEEK: FORTY-NINERS TO WIN BY 1-4 POINTS (+350)

As stated above I already have a much larger bet on the Niners to win by 3.5 or more. This was my hedge just in case they were to win by a field goal or less. After the Falcons burned me by a half a point in the NFC title game, I am sensitive to half-points here and there. This eliminates that problem completely. If the Niners win the game, I win something. With the long payout, I can bet a small amount and hedge a large portion of a much bigger bet on the spread.

Of course, there is also a best case scenario where the Niners win by exactly four (which sounds familiar for some reason) and I win both bets.

Regardless of whether I win any of these bets, it will be a bittersweet win. It would be nice to go out with a win obviously, but even with a win, I am still stepping off the ride one last time.

Even before I came to Las Vegas and immersed myself in sports gambling 24x7, I looked at the Super Bowl through the prism of gambling – especially since it has now been fourteen years since the Broncos made the game. I would spend the week leading to the game reading about crazy prop bets and putting together betting pools with friends on the day of the game with a free dinner as stakes. With hours of build-up on the day itself, something above and beyond listening to five ex-players discuss the same over-analyzed storylines is necessary to avoid going insane.

Even this year, with at least a modicum of rooting interest with the Niners in the game, the game is still defined for me by gambling. Yes, I would be happy if the Niners win but I would be REALLY happy if they win by four or more. Throw in the myriad of prop bets and a decent sized Total bet and I will spend the day as conflicted as a Log Cabin Republican while I try to determine which bet I should be cheering on at any given moment. But this is the last chance to bet on football this season, so it is absolutely time to go all out.

Will I make a killing on the game? Probably not. If I have learned anything, I will probably win a few bets, and lose a few more with the only determinant of profit being that I win the big bets and lose the small bets.

Ultimately though, it doesn't really matter. I have lost nowhere near the amount I prepared to lose this season and am not the biggest fan of the options available for the game, so while I will have more bet on the game than any other game this season, it won't be so much that I will be selling my hair if I lose. I will (almost assuredly) end the season with a bankroll down but not catastrophically down.

This game will have moments of fandom stress and it will have moments of sports-bettor stress for me but in the end it will be defined by emotion. Specifically, sadness. This marks the end of the ride for me. On Monday morning, the restraint raises, I stand up and disembark from the roller coaster. I am not returning to work (or even Denver) immediately but wandering around the amusement park for the next month and a half. However, it just won't be the same with my favorite ride now closed.

So I guess I need to savor every moment of this last run around the track. Even if my stomach drops a few times as the cart falls out from underneath me, I need to remind myself to enjoy the momentary nausea. In a week, I will desperately miss every moment, even the disappointing ones.

♪♪♪

In the end, the NFL got exactly the Super Bowl they wanted.

The game was exciting--full of big plays and suspense. Even the thirty minute black-out ended up being a blessing when it flipped the script from a blow-out to shootout. The game came down to the final moments and when the clock hit 0:00, the NFL's Cinderella wasn't turned into a pumpkin but rather into a football deity to put on a pedestal (or TV studio chair) and admire. When NFL Films captures this film in the future for one of those 30-minute Super Bowl summaries I so loved as a child it will be all about one of the game's greats going out a champion. The myth will be complete.

Of course, like any myth there is a lot more to the story. But that also makes this game perfect for the NFL. This game was the ultimate one-game encapsulation of the NFL – the myth that Roger Goodell and his sycophants in the media want you to believe and the much uglier truth they wipe off their $1,000 loafers on the way to the box seats.

The NFL and the media have embraced the Ray Lewis narrative throughout the playoffs. Even quite literally on occasion.

They have pushed the 'great, godly warrior' narrative constantly for weeks. Yet it is the Ray Lewis story they don't acknowledge that is a greater personification of the NFL. A man that was arrested in connection with the murder of two men and was reported to have been using PEDs last week is now the Ultimate Champion. The man who single-handedly willed his team to a Super Bowl win.

This wasn't just Ray Lewis' Super Bowl, it was also Roger Goodell's.

Ignoring off-field crimes and PED-use in the pursuit of a myth to sell the public is the very definition of the NFL business model today. That he was helped by incompetent refs – or maybe refs that got the memo that this was Ray Lewis' Super Bowl – who willfully ignored obvious penalties that they have called all season, as well as helmet to helmet hits that the NFL swears need to be removed from the game just makes it a more complete picture.

But for this week the center of that myth was Ray Lewis. I mostly ignored the hours of pre-game leading up to the show because I don't need to listen to large, old men talk about nothing and laugh too much but I did catch Shannon Sharpe's interview with Ray-Ray before the game. No one is ever going to confuse Shannon with any sort of journalist but in one moment he gave us the clearest view of Ray Lewis that we may ever see.

Shannon, to his credit as a former teammate and presumed friend, asked Ray Lewis what he had to say to the families of the two men that died in the stabbing incident in 2000 for which Lewis was subsequently arrested. Lewis' answer rambled and stammered and ultimately said very little but what I took from its mangling of coherent sentences were the two fundamental facts Lewis seems to believe about that night.

(1) Lewis says 'God makes no mistakes' which I take to mean he believes those two men deserved to die

(2) He also then talked about being prosecuted (or in his mind persecuted) because of who he is, not what he did.

In essence, Ray Lewis looks at an incident when two men died and sees himself as the victim. It was the type of bizarre, ludicrous and delusional response that comes when someone has lied to himself (or been lied to by others) for so long that he no longer has a grasp on the reality of the situation. The facts have been molded to fit what he now wants or needs to believe.

We have seen a lot of that lately – just ask Lance Armstrong and Manti Te'o.

The ironic thing is that after years of his defenders ignoring his off-field actions by lauding his on-field greatness, it was his on-field play that could have been the cause of greater embarrassment. Let's face it, Ray Lewis got abused in the Super Bowl. He couldn't have covered a drunk stumbling out of Pat O'Brien's last night. On the rare occasion he got near a ball carrier they blasted through his arm tackles. Apparently he needed to take a fourth hit of Deer Antler Spray before the game, because three wasn't enough.

If Ray Lewis were half of the leader he pretends to be when a camera is nearby he would have benched himself because his inability to keep up with Forty-Niner running backs and tight ends nearly cost the Ravens the game.

But Lewis could never do something selfless for his team because this wasn't about his team. This was about him and the myth of his greatness that he has built up in his head. There will be no comeuppance for him. He will now go get paid millions by one of the NFL's partners to talk about himself and his God in place of the football game he is supposed to be analyzing and all his co-hosts will just chuckle. He will be a legend to be rhapsodized about over soaring string music and slow-motion replays for years to come. The story is complete, now it is time for it to become legend.

And legends in Roger Goodell's NFL have no place for inconvenient truths.

➤➤➤

I remember reading Jimmy Buffett once talking about how he hates New Year's Eve because he thinks of it as 'amateur night'; anyone that thinks they are a musician plays on New Year's Eve. The same could be said for going out on New Year's Eve. Every man and woman – people who only sip alcohol once a year – end up going out somewhere on New Year's Eve; it is amateur night for party goers as well.

For gamblers, the Super Bowl is New Year's Eve. Everyone wants to bet on THE BIG GAME. People who have yet to bet all season lay large sums of money solely because it is the culmination of the NFL season. Whether they know anything or not, if they are part of the half that got lucky and bet on the winner, they spend the rest of the year convinced they are some sort of gambling genius--convinced their real calling in life is to be a professional gambler.

Given the laws in the U.S., all of those bettors have only one place to come to place those bets: Las Vegas. Whereas on any other weekend I had my choice of locations for watching games, it is nearly impossible to just walk in somewhere and watch the Super Bowl. Most casinos host special viewing parties by either invitation only or by paying an exorbitant fee (I saw prices ranging from $50 to $100 just to walk in the door). Even the Hard Rock, where a month earlier I had no problem reserving ten seats for the BCS National Championship game only allowed individuals possessing Cantor accounts with more than $1,000 in it to reserve a seat. And that got you one seat. Rodney and his wife, Heather, came into town to watch the game and be here for my grand finale, so even my single account couldn't get us enough seats.

On the day before the game, I met Rodney at the LVH. Upon entering the sports book, we saw the betting line wind from the betting windows up stairs and partway into the main casino floor. When you are known for your broad menu of 300+ prop bets, everyone stops in to throw some money down in the days leading up to the game. After standing in line for thirty minutes, we laid a few prop bets for fun and then proceeded next door to the theater that houses Football Central on Sundays all fall.

On this evening, it was hosting the world premiere of a movie entitled *Life On the Line*, a documentary that followed around several pro bettors in the days leading up to the Super Bowl in 2011. After the documentary, I ran into Jay Kornegay and asked him for advice on watching the game. Knowing that Football Central opens in the early afternoon, I wanted to know when he recommended arriving to ensure seats. Instead, he graciously offered VIP seats for the three of us, letting us skip the line and enjoy free food and drink.

Super Bowl Sunday, after a greasy breakfast, the three of us arrived back at the LVH around noon. Immediately getting back in the betting window line, twenty minutes later we had laid some last minute bets for friends back home tardy in placing their requests.

Walking across the casino to the entrance for Football Central, a line of fans stretched along the wall as far as we could see – a full three hours before kick-off. Unsure of the process, we walked toward the back, only it bent around the corner down another hallway and didn't end until it reached a conference room – it literally ran out of room. We got in line, still unsure of the process and waited for the doors to open. Shortly after 1:00 p.m., the line started slowly moving, but so slowly I grew impatient. I jumped out of line to check whether our VIP bracelets earned us a separate dedicated entry. Sure enough, we hopped out of line and walked right in, securing our own row of three seats in the balcony but with two hours to kill until kick-off. Over those two hours the balcony slowly filled until pretty much every seat was filled.

Once kick-off came, our viewing experience was like any other large public viewing. Forty-Niner fans easily out-numbered Ravens fans but every drive garnered cheers from somewhere in the theater. There is no point in re-capping the game. If you have read this far, you watched the game. And if you read my pre-game picks above you know I didn't win much on the game. But I did learn some things.

I have spent this season educating myself about sports gambling – fighting my way down the path to becoming a Wiseguy. Each week I have learned a new lesson that I incorporate into my mindset going forward, so it is only fitting that in the biggest betting weekend of the year I learned two lessons important for anyone to follow if they truly want to be a sharp bettor.

First, never get wrapped up in the 'eventness' of a game and end up betting more than your system says you should.

As with most things in life, lessons aren't learned in triumph – no one learned how hot a stove burner is by not touching it. Lessons are learned in defeat. I lost significant money on the Super Bowl. I lost too much even for someone who handicapped the game completely incorrectly.

I can lament the missed calls by the refs, or the fact that apparently the only thing that Ray Lewis' God loves more than cheaters and hypocrites are hail mary passes, but I won't. Instead, I will take some blame myself (one thing that Ray Lewis' God apparently dislikes). This was the ultimate example of why anyone that wants to be a professional or long term gambler needs discipline.

In my handicapping of the game I projected a spread and Over/Under very close to those being offered by the casinos. There was little value. Yet, given this was the grand finale to the season, I bet heavily regardless. Between large bets on the Forty-Niners and the Under, coupled with a multitude of small prop bets, I had significantly more money bet on this game, than any single game all season. With little value I should have bet small or looked for hedges, yet I didn't. I went full-bore with what I expected to happen.

It is easy to lay thousands of dollars when you come to Las Vegas once a year for the game. You can show up for the game and feel like a big deal – especially if you flipped the coin and it landed on the correct side. It is a completely different animal to bet every week. The only way to win consistently is to govern the size of your bets based on your confidence level. Just because a game is the final one of the college or pro season doesn't mean you should bet more. Especially if your handicapping system has thrown up its hands and told you 'your guess is as good as mine.'

So I lost a lot. In fact, the only bets I won were the small bets I laid just in case the game didn't go as I expected, which is never a good thing.

But it was this outcome that leads to the second lesson for the aspiring wiseguy: don't let a bet's result impact your approach – there is always another game to move on to.

On Saturday afternoon when Rodney and I went to see the movie about professional gamblers, we were a short walk from the long line of bettors, but a greater contrast couldn't have been drawn. While amateur hour reigned outside--people making their out-sized once-a-year bet--the movie showed the small set of men that make their entire living by gambling. While they all laid bets on the Super Bowl (bets bigger than 95% of the public), there was nothing special for them. It was just another game to bet on. In fact, if anything it was the opposite – with so much attention it is hard to imagine finding a lot of value. One of the gamblers (I don't recall which) admitted in the movie he actually keeps his Super Bowl bets (relatively) small. Like virtually none of the people standing in line outside, the Super Bowl isn't the end of the betting year for these guys. It is just time to transition to the next sport – NBA, college basketball, NHL.

This is the final lesson that I need to learn to continue my progression from pure public bettor to being at least a "wise-guy like substance." A loss can't be obsessed about. A loss needs to be forgotten in preparation for the next bet. It is always onward and upward for pro bettors. A cold streak is to be endured with the confidence that a hot streak is on its way.

One of the wiseguys in the movie, while acknowledging he lost money on his Super Bowl bets, actually felt positive because he believed his system and approach had been validated. Unlike someone looking at a team failing to convert a 4th down as proof they shouldn't have gone for it, wiseguys know that outcomes can't dictate what was the correct decision. A wiseguy focuses on process rather than outcome. A missed call by a ref. A shanked field goal. An unfortunate fumble. A gambler can't control every aspect of a game--the most they can do is follow their approach and maximize their chances of winning. A loss needs to be shrugged off in pursuit of the bigger goal. Lose a battle but win the war.

There is no such thing as a bad taste in the mouth of a pro bettor. Money lost today can always be won back tomorrow. While it is an admirable trait and a professional necessity for wiseguys, unfortunately for me that isn't quite the case.

While this season I started on the journey to becoming a gambler more educated than most, my time dedicated to betting football has come to an end. I didn't quite complete the journey before the season closed on me. Trace elements of amateur bettor still inhabit my DNA.

I will spend the off-season kicking myself for over-betting and figuring out how to improve my system. I need this time to gain some distance before coming back and laying money on the NFL again next fall.

But, in the meantime, while I am still in Las Vegas, I can continue progressing down the road to wiseguyville.

After all, I won an NBA bet the night after the Super Bowl.

A small bet, because I wasn't overly confident in it.